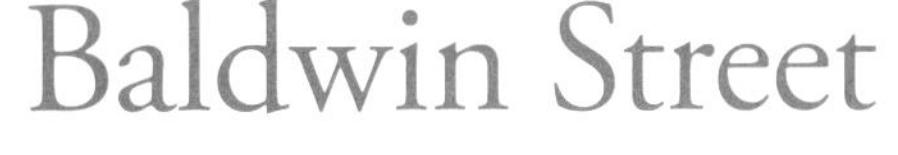
Baldwin Street

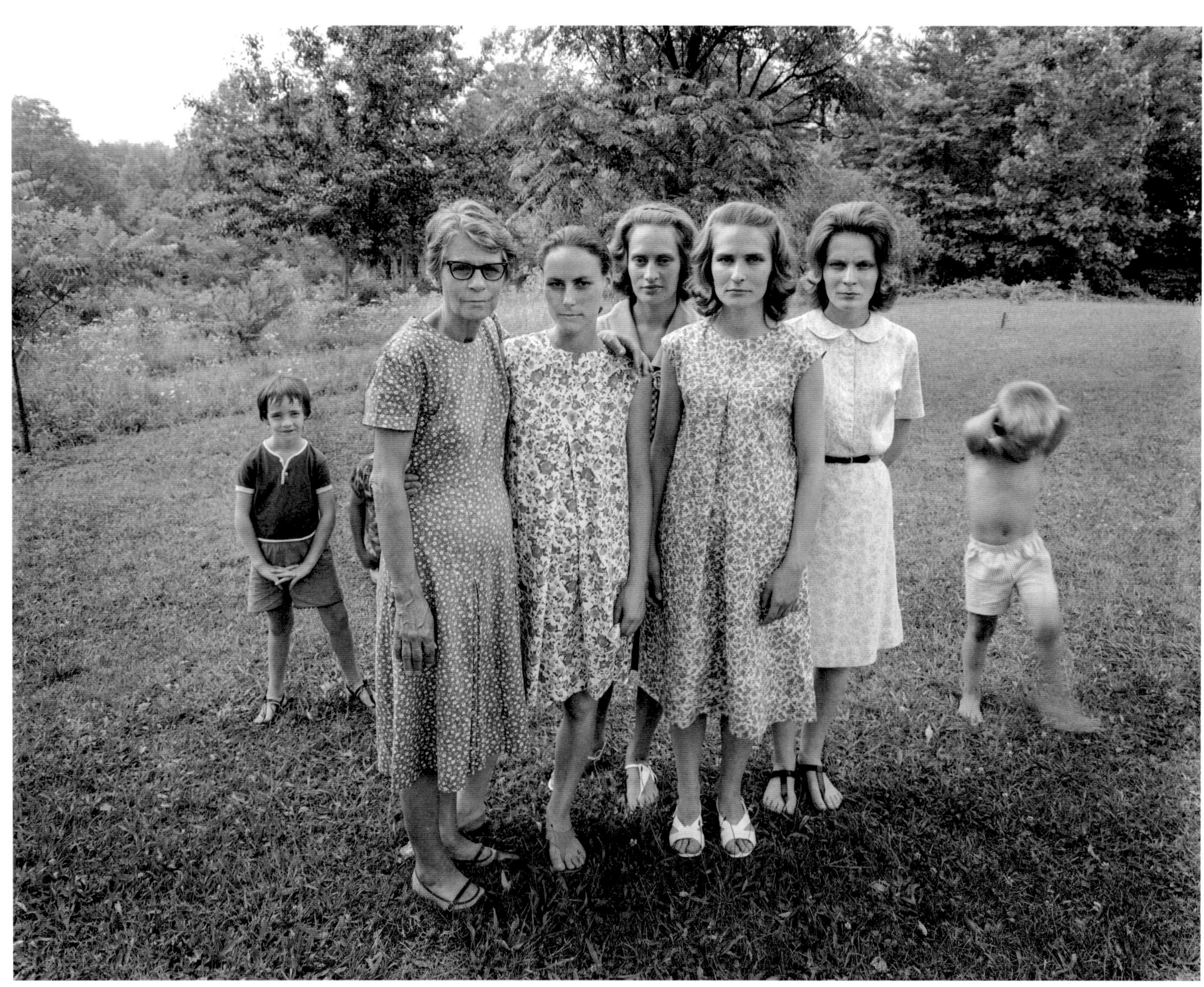

Nancy, Reva, Edith, Ruth, Mae, Helen, and Dwayne, Danville, 1967

Baldwin Street

Photographs 1966–1994

Emmet Gowin

PRINCETON UNIVERSITY PRESS
PRINCETON AND OXFORD

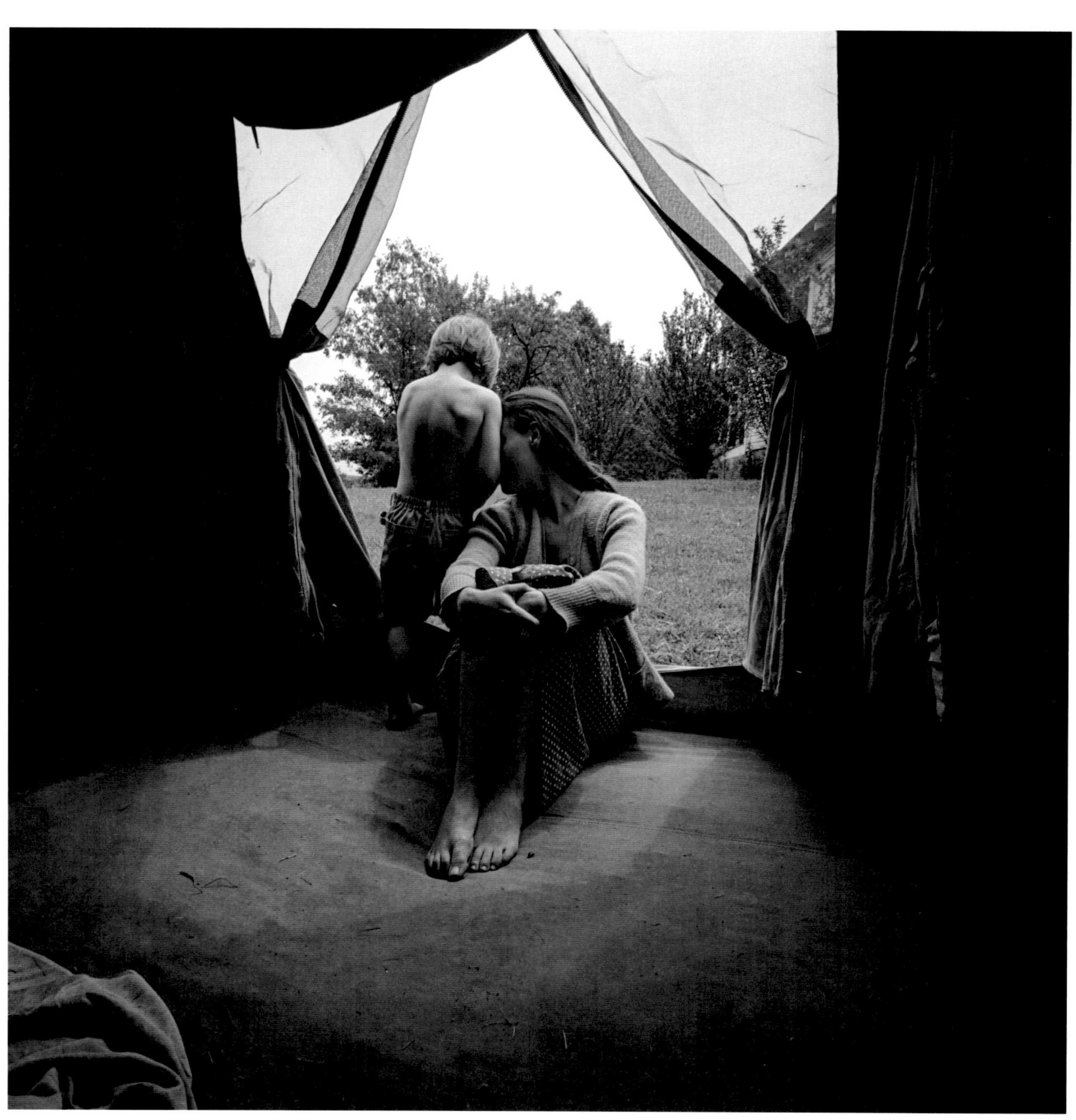

Edith and Elijah, May 1971

Baldwin Street Photographs 1966–1994

Through my marriage to Edith Morris, in 1964, I entered a family freshly different from my own. I admired their simplicity and generosity and thought of the pictures I made as agreements. I wanted to pay attention to the body and personality that had agreed out of love to reveal itself. My attention was a natural duty that could honor that love.

Danville takes its name from the Dan River and sits on the rolling southern Piedmont border of Virginia and North Carolina. The John and Reva Morris family lived at the bottom of Baldwin Street, which sits at the far western edge of a cotton mill town, Danville, Virginia. Danville was home to Dan River Mills and was self-proclaimed as the "World's Best" tobacco market. Today, Danville is better known as the "Last Capital of the Confederacy."

The bottom of Baldwin Street came to a dead end, embraced then by a circle of low woods. It was here that the city itself seemed to disappear and time seemed less important. By 1960, what had been Frederick Booher's market garden and grazing fields were almost all overgrown. The last five or six houses on Baldwin Street also formed a half circle and belonged to members of this extended family, including the grown children of Fred and Rennie Booher. Reva Booher Morris, one of five daughters, and Edith's mother lived in the last house on the right. For over fifty years, those houses and yards, along with Reva's garden on Baldwin Street, all the children, the aunts and uncles, that small but intensely vivid and inspiring world, was in my mind the true center of the world. The kingdom of heaven seemed to be all around us, everywhere I looked. Through Edith and her family, Baldwin Street became the center of my spiritual universe.

Edith Morris was born on Baldwin Street. Between 1940 and 1943, John and Reva Morris had four girls; Mae, Ruth, Edith, and Helen. Only later did I learn that even before I knew there was an Edith, her family knew my family. My father had for two years pastored a Methodist church at the top of the hill, on the old Martinsville Road, which Edith's mother, Reva, told me they regularly attended.

In December 1960, a friend, who also played football for the high school, asked me to tag along to the YWCA Saturday Night Dance. There was someone he wanted me to meet. "There she is," Jim said. I watched Edith dance for a few minutes and then the contest was over. I think she won the contest but even if she didn't, I was clear about one thing: this was the most alive person I'd ever met. By Christmas I was selling things I treasured to buy Edith a first present. We dated for almost four years and married in 1964, just before my last year in art school. Over all these years, Edith has been my guide and informant in all things, especially on the subject of life and Baldwin Street.

Most of the photographs in *Baldwin Street* have not been published before. Many were only printed for the first time during the pandemic of 2020–2022. Some images I knew were authentic even when I was young, and others I recognized only once the negatives were rediscovered. Until then, I simply did not have the skill or the right frame of mind to print most of them. As I look back, the key family years were 1963–1978, but I never lost interest in the gestures or the faces of this dearest of families. It was here that I came of age and found my first true subject.

Emmet Gowin October 3, 2025

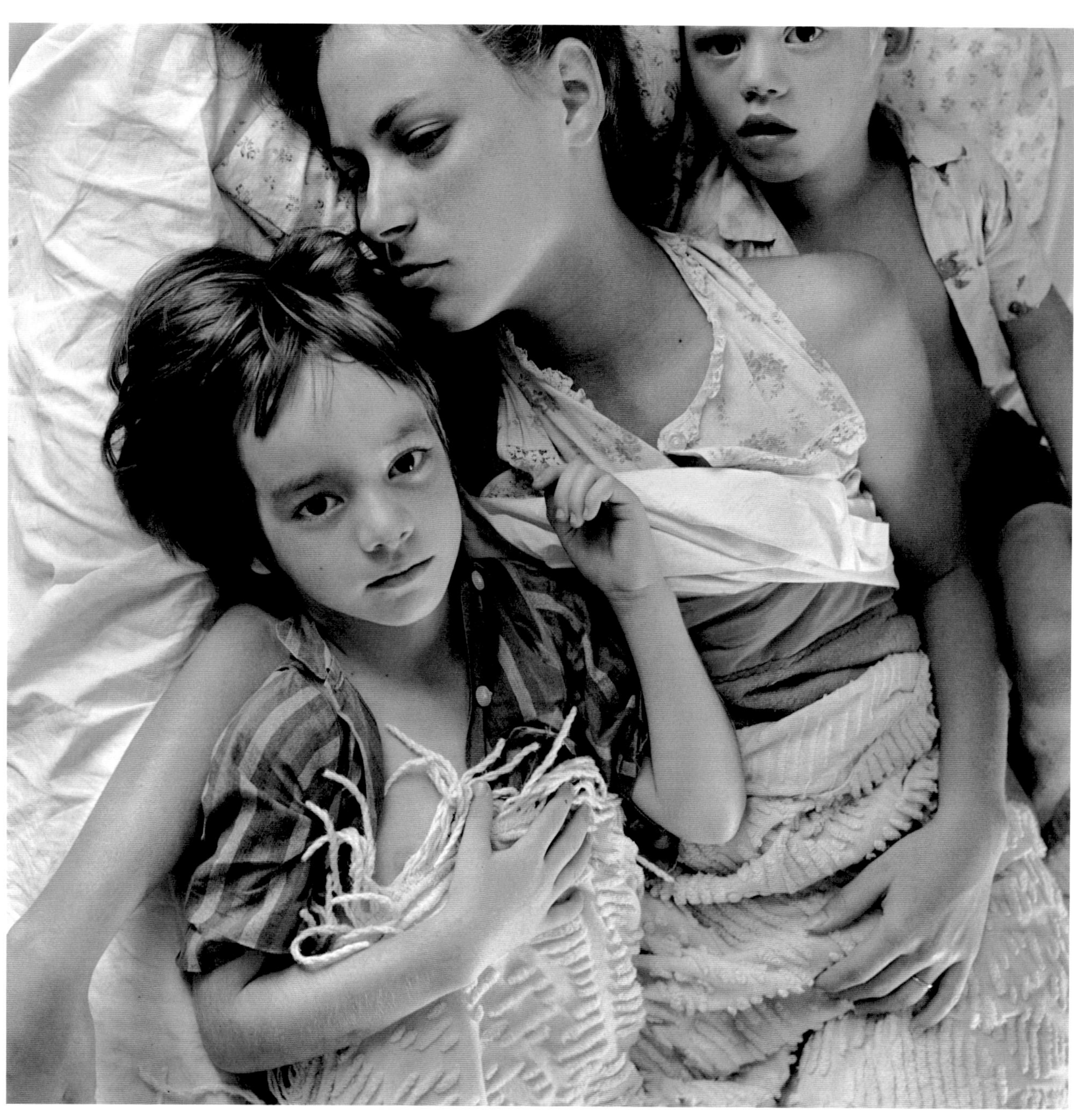

Nancy, Edith, and Dwayne, Danville, 1966

Conversation with Edith and Emmet Gowin

COLLECTED AND EDITED BY JOEL SMITH

EMMET Edith, do you remember how the children would get into bed in the morning? They wouldn't even wait for you to wake up. They would just come and sort of slither under the covers.

EDITH *Well, that happened almost daily with one child or the other. And we didn't have children then.*

EMMET Edith's mother was taking care of two grandchildren, Ruth's children. And whenever Edith was around, they would sort of cling to her like their own mother. They would find the same comfort in her, the same physicality, that we later saw with our own children.

I'm sure this is 1966. It's the first winter we drove home from Rhode Island to be in Virginia for Christmas. We were there until the first days of the New Year, then we drove back when school started up again. Maggie would often give Edith five dollars to keep us "safe on the road."

EDITH *My mom, Reva, began her family late in life. She must have been around thirty-eight or thirty-nine when I was born. She probably was called an old maid up until she began her family. Mae was born first, Ruth number two, Edith number three, and Helen number four. Helen was born on my first birthday. Three of us were born in November, one year apart.*

EMMET Reva had been married once before and had twins who didn't survive. It wasn't so uncommon in that time that families would start out and it didn't work. The same was true of Reva's sister Maggie. Besides her one child that we knew, she'd had two children that we didn't know about, who'd died soon after birth. They died of a blood defect, little understood at the time, the Rh-negative factor, which can now be corrected before birth.

Edith and her family lived at the bottom of Baldwin Street. That was about five miles out of town on the old Martinsville Road. I was born a year before Edith, in a house only a mile away—but over the next fifteen years we moved seven times as my father, a minister, was reassigned to churches throughout Virginia. In 1957 my family returned to Danville, but to the far, northern, side of town. Danville is divided by the river, south and north. North Danville must have been the auxiliary or newer part of the city. It was up a steep hill, and we lived up at the top. The city's downtown was on a more gradual hill, going south. The bridges were placed exactly where the fords and bridges had been during the Civil War.

I finished high school in 1959 and went straight into business school. I was in my second year when I met Edith. I think I was nineteen. I saw Edith dancing, and I guess I asked for her phone number. I started calling, and we started talking. But it was a while before we dated.

EDITH *You were very different than all the other young men. They would all do the same hangouts. They would go to the same hamburger joint. They would go to the same dance on Saturday night. But not you. When I started seeing you, you wanted to go get a hamburger and a hot dog at a stand where the man who ran it also collected coins, like you. And you would talk about what coins you needed, and stamps. And that was what our date was. Not going to hang out, but to go see somebody about your interest in coins.*

EMMET Well, it was business, too, because I was trading coins with the owner.

EDITH *I graduated high school in 1961. When I grew up, you weren't expected to go to college. When you graduated from high school, that was the ultimate. You had a party and everybody was so excited that you were finished.*

EMMET Once business school was finished, Edith and I began to discuss my applying to Richmond Professional Institute. I had always drawn as a child and now I wanted to study art. Edith was very positive and said she would work in Danville until I graduated.

By the first weekend I came home from art school, probably October 1961, I'd learned how to load a two-and-a-quarter Yashica camera and process roll film. There are very few pictures left from that time, but some are of Edith.

I met Edith's mother the first time I went to the house. I probably didn't meet many other people until I finally started picking Edith up with the car. I felt excited about the family from the very first meeting. Driving down the street in my father's old 1952 Chrysler, I remember how that felt. It was like turning back time. The bottom of Baldwin Street didn't look like a farm. It was just a collection of houses at the edge of town. But as you went down the hill to the dead end, it was culturally different. And I felt so in tune with it. I think I probably identified it with my own grandfather, Elijah.

And I immediately adored and admired Edith's mother. Reva's relationship with her daughters was so admirable, and I quickly realized that there was a sort of matriarchal cluster here, where the things that had to be done were being done by the women.

Edith's father had died in an automobile accident in 1952. Men were there—Willie Cooper lived next door with Maggie, and Raymond Booher lived two houses up, married to Verlie, and they had kids. And the men were good at telling stories and sitting around and drinking coffee. But the women were doing what seemed to me the real work. The women were all weavers in the cotton mill. They were weaving broadcloth and sheeting and gingham fabric.

EDITH *I never worked at the mill. The only sister that worked there was Ruth.*

You know, you could make money in the cotton mill. If you were a farmer, it was a struggle. You never knew when your crops were going to be good, or not. In the cotton mill, you knew what kind of salary you were going to have. So it was more secure; you didn't have to worry about it. And it was more than you made if you worked with your family in a market garden. My grandfather, Reva's dad, was a peddler of meats, fish, and vegetables. Every summer he had a garden, and with his horse and wagon he would go to the mill or around the neighborhood selling his produce.

Emmet and I now live in my grandmother's house each summer.

EMMET It's the house where many, many of our photographs were taken. I think it was the first house on Baldwin Street. It was at the very bottom, on a kind of promontory where two creeks formed a ridge. Edith's grandfather had farmed the sides of that hill and the flatter ground around it. Then Reva built a house. Gertrude built a house that she never did live in, and built another house up the road, which somebody else lived in. Maggie built a house. Raymond built a house.

EDITH *So it was five or six houses that were family or belonged to somebody in the family.*

The menu in our house was always very simple. It was beans, particularly pintos, cornbread, and once a week chicken, and maybe a vegetable from the garden. And I think my mother felt this was so meager that she felt bad about offering it to you for dinner. But it didn't take too long before she got over that.

EMMET After we married, Reva would say, "Well, what do you want for supper?" And I'd say, "Well, let me make it." She would have the front of the yard plowed every spring, and on spring break we'd be off for a week and I would plant a garden. And then she would take care of it until summer. And for ten, fifteen years, we'd come back and she'd finish the garden out.

EDITH *My sister Mae, the oldest one, got married when she was just eighteen, and her husband's family were moving to Southern California. So Mae was the first person in the family who didn't live within thirty miles. It was quite a shock. And my sister Ruth married when she was young, probably eighteen as well. She lived a couple of doors up from us. And mom took care of Ruth's children. Nancy was born in 1960 and Dwayne in 1962.*

What did the family make of Emmet? They thought that he was kind. They thought that he was of a different class. He was known by the family as "Dr. Gowin's son, dating Edith. Oh, my. Isn't that wonderful?" It was very different, that he was dating a mill worker's daughter. Emmet's mother was a Quaker and she went to Friends Bible College in Haviland, Kansas, and she graduated in music. She was educated. Nobody in our family had been to college at that point. I had been dating young people that I didn't know what kind of class they were. But my family knew the difference between a mill worker's family and somebody that was educated. My sisters to this day love him. They love that he is exciting, that he talks about things that they never thought about. He goes and looks at things in the woods and brings back things to talk about. And he was like that from the beginning.

EMMET Well, I knew my trees and plants pretty good. Because I had to know them to get those merit badges in Scouts. You know, you got to do your homework.

EDITH *He was just exciting and fun to be with. If they saw him with his camera, photographing, they would invite him to come over and talk about what he was doing. And they liked being photographed by him. That's the short answer.*

EMMET We married in August 1964, with my senior year at Richmond Professional Institute still ahead of me. As soon as we married, when we left the church, we got in the car and went to Richmond, two or three weeks ahead of school starting. And once school started it was pretty steady. That was a hard year for Edith because she was working, with not so many people to talk to.

EDITH *After moving to Richmond, I worked there for an attorney, and it was very boring sitting all day long, typing. You never met anybody, you just sat at this little office. And I'd never lived in a city before. You'd look out the window and it was just cement or brick. And I was used to grass, I was used to my sisters and family. So no, I was a very lonely person that year.*

Before that, I was in Danville. Volkswagens had just come to the U.S., and in Danville I worked for the Harville Motor Company that had switched from selling Mack trucks to selling VWs. And when I became a secretary there, I would meet people. The excitement of all those VWs coming from Germany: it was the place to be.

EMMET Then in 1965 we moved to Rhode Island, and the first real family images came on visits to Danville in '65. When I say "real," I mean with the big camera, formal pictures, and almost knowing what I was doing. I had been taking my Leica around and snapping things all over the place, but it didn't seem quite real. It does seem sort of *half* real now: as I go looking for these two-and-a-quarter negatives, I find the 35-millimeters that I filed in the same way. But I don't pore over those, thinking there's some mystery here that I didn't see.

The family pictures really began when I was accepted at Rhode Island School of Design. Harry Callahan told the graduate students—there were just three of us—"Well, fellas, you're all grown up now. Why don't you just work on the projects that come to your mind, and in a month we'll get together and look at what you've done." We were shocked by that, but it also meant that Edith and I had time together. By now we had been living together for a year. When we had time, when she wasn't working, we'd get in the car and go somewhere for the day, and that was a chance to make pictures.

Then a galvanizing thing happened. Within that first month in Providence I got a draft notice, saying come to Danville at five in the morning on the twenty-fifth of October for induction into the army. I thought, I didn't sign up for that; I don't want to be in the army or in Vietnam. So within maybe a day, I called the draft board and arranged to visit. I drove back to Virginia to explain that I considered myself a conscientious objector and to ask, could I apply for that status? And that was a life-changing moment in many ways. I stayed with Edith's mother, and she had Nancy and Dwayne. And the children would be around me the same way they would be around Edith. The way kids attach to young adults is understandable; it's a hunger, a natural thing. And that's when Nancy said, "You're taking too many pictures of my cousin; how about taking some pictures of me? I'm going to think of some good things for you to photograph."

When I got back from the draft board, I showed Callahan that first picture, of Nancy with her dolls, which had been her idea and her arrangement. He said, think of this as your first picture. That was very liberating, because I realized: that's Nancy's idea, that's her. If I hadn't followed her advice, if I had fought her about that, nothing would have happened. You just have to give in to what the world has to offer.

We were there in Providence for two years, and the best pictures would come about when I would go to Virginia.

EDITH *Our houses were so small. The house that I grew up in had four rooms: two bedrooms, a living room, and a kitchen. If you had your extended family there every day, it could be four, five, ten people. And if it was warm outside, you spent your time outdoors, not in that hot little wooden house.*

The afternoon sun focused on Reva's front porch, so the porch was hot and no salvation. In the evening, we would all go behind the house under a tree and prepare dinner—peel potatoes, shuck beans and corn and so forth—outside. You'd go into the kitchen to cook, and you'd endure it, but it was hot. So when we're seeing the table outside and the chairs and so on, it's because life was really going on out there on the grass.

During the day everyone was busy with whatever they do—wash, clean, have an extra cup of coffee with your spouse. But in the evening, in the spring, summer, and fall, they would gather on the porch. Everyone had their own chairs. I now have my grandmother's chair. Nobody sits in my rocking chair. I don't sit in my sisters' chairs when they come around. My aunts would all sit in their chairs all across the porch and talk about the day. If not much had gone on in the day, they would talk about what happened last week or last year. Now my sisters and I, every day, will sit out on the porch with our coffee and talk. All the interconnections of people seem simple. And yet, if you really delve into it with your own life, there's a lot of depth there—solving problems or looking at things in a way you never thought about.

EMMET There's four funerals involved in these pictures, 1971, 1972, 1973, and 1976. The 1971 funeral is my grandfather Elijah's. They lived their whole lives in Buckingham County, near Appomattox Court House. When I was young and didn't understand much about the Civil War, I conflated grandfather's mailing address in Andersonville, Virginia, with Andersonville, Georgia, and the camp where Union prisoners were held. I thought, my God, there's no sign of a prison camp here. But a little later we went to Spotsylvania Court House in the summer for a holiness camp meeting that my father was on the board of. That area was also the battleground site of Spotsylvania: "The Bloody Angle." And Chancellorsville was not far away. It was just a vortex in the Civil War. Sometimes, in Virginia, we felt haunted by that war, just as Vietnam haunted our youth. In contrast with that, here on Baldwin Street was this amazing clan of women who nurtured life, and kept children safe, and embraced us for who we were.

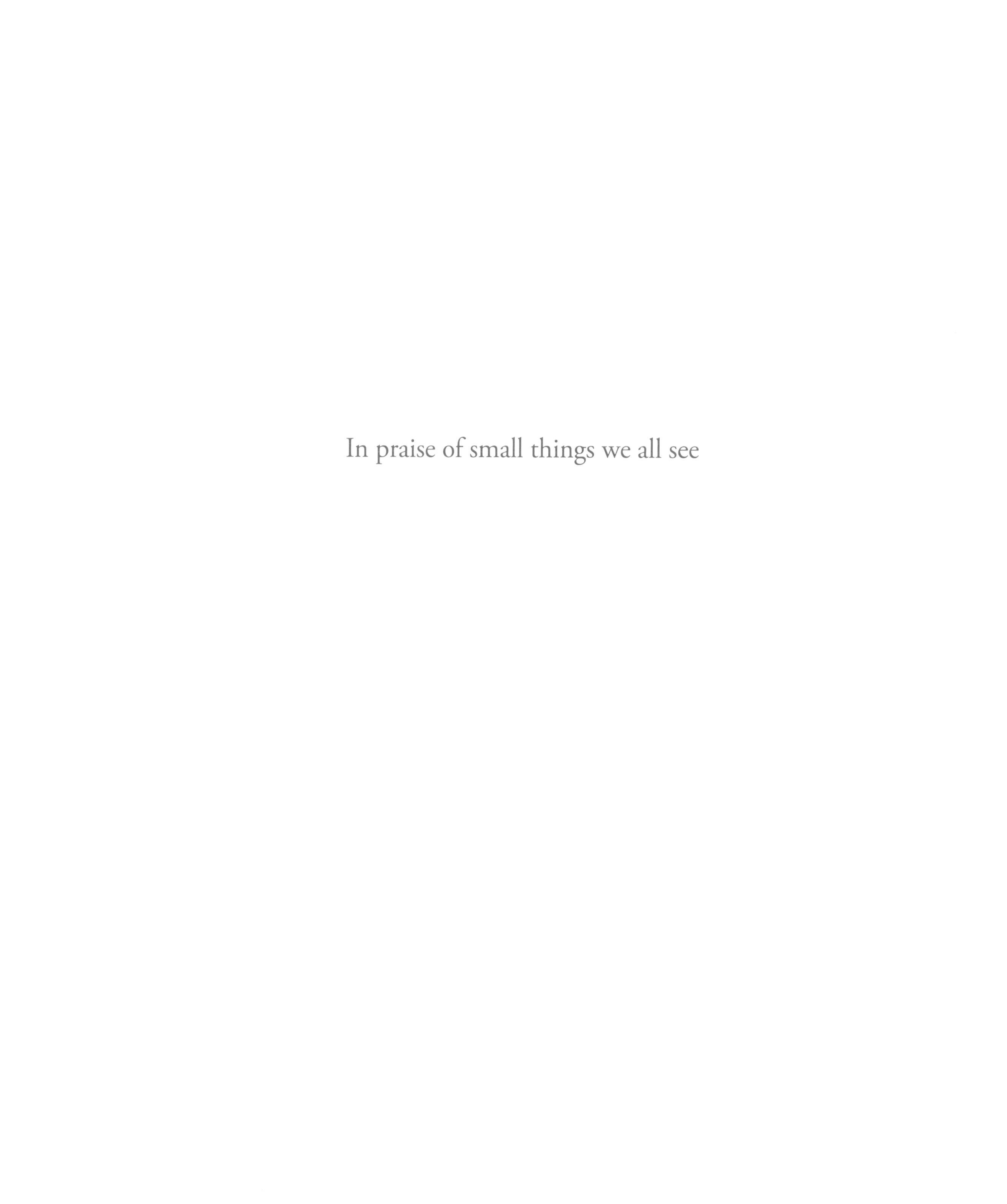

In praise of small things we all see

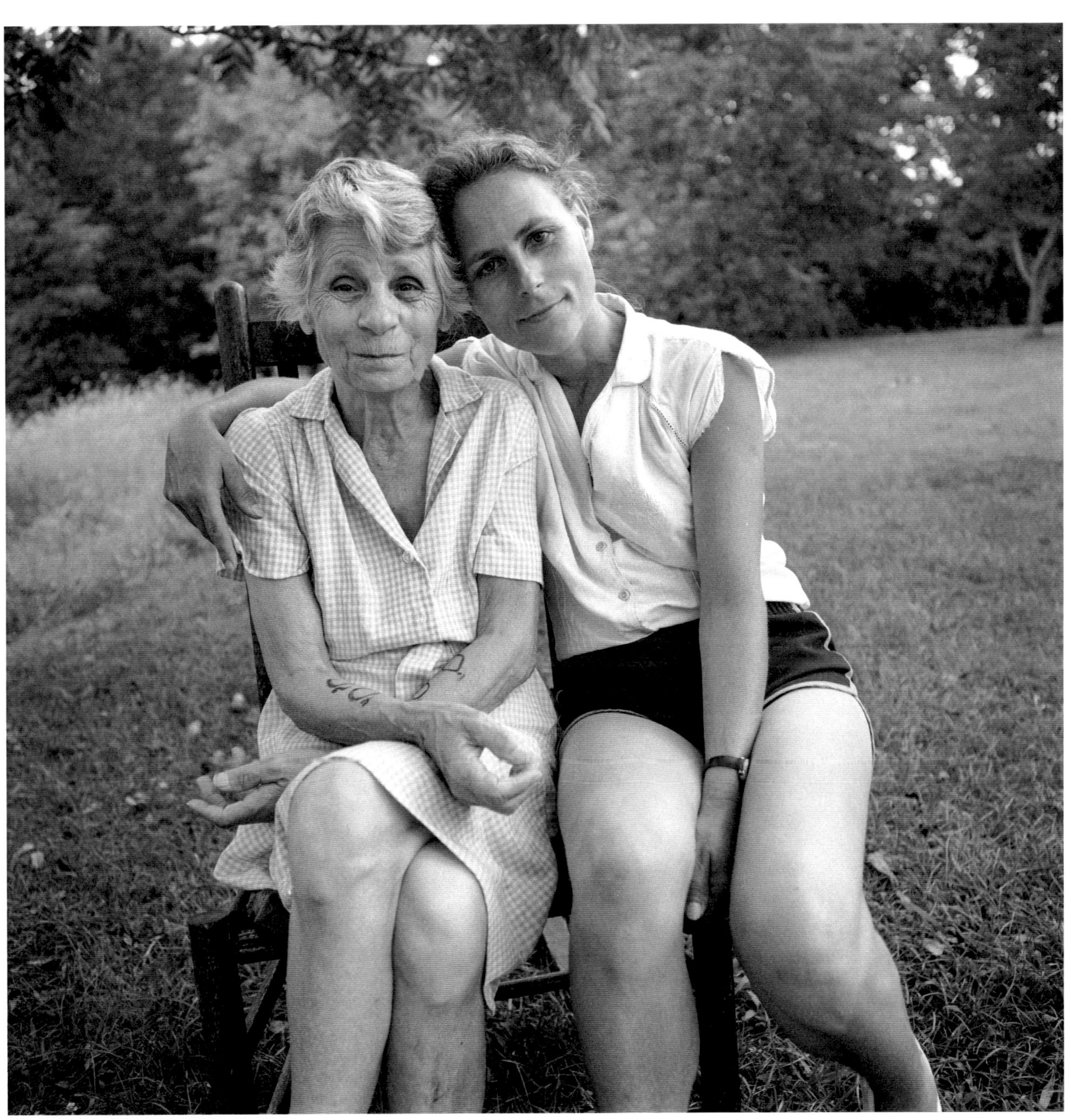

Reva and Edith, Danville, 1984

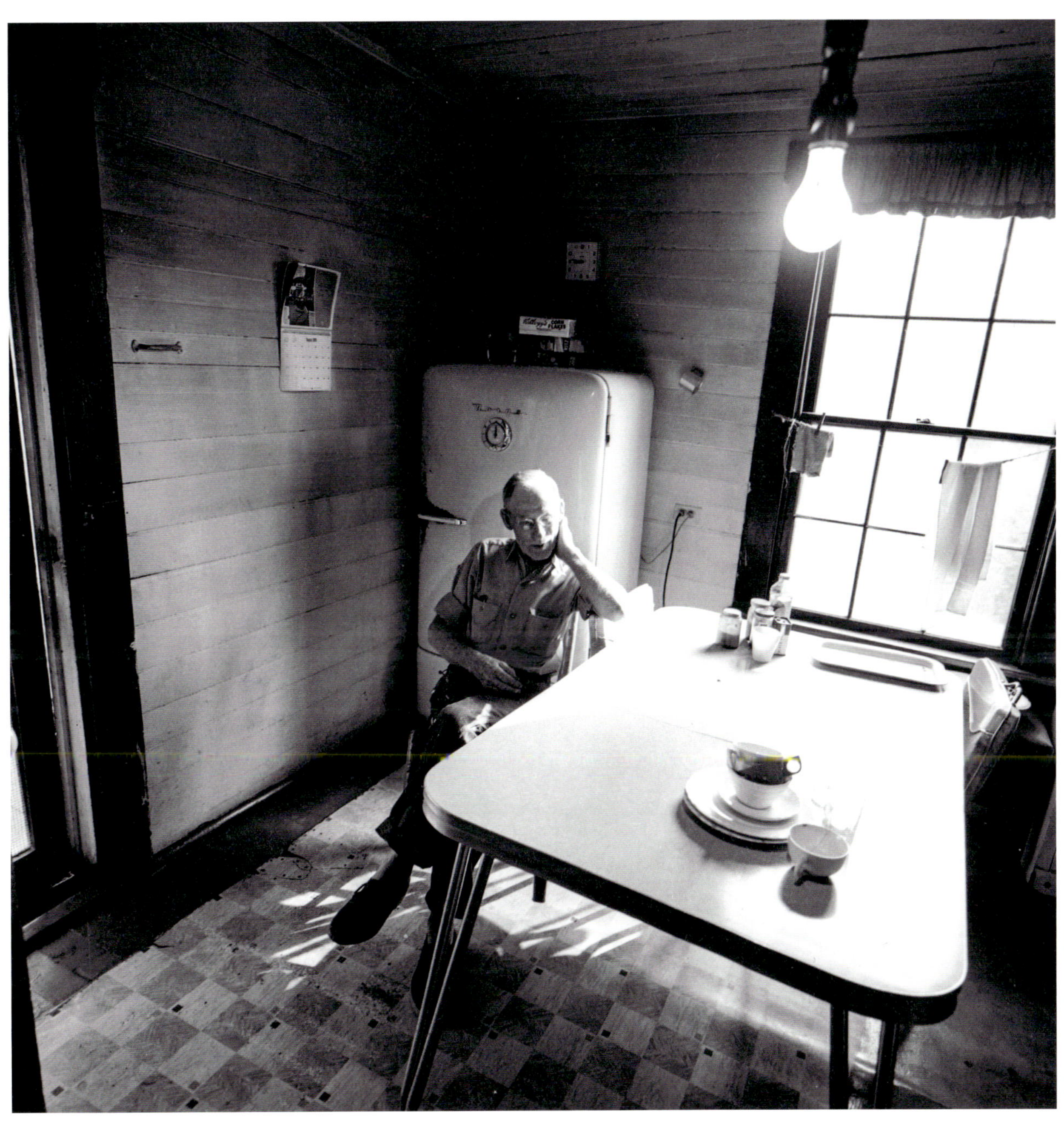

Raymond in his Mother's Kitchen, Danville, 1970

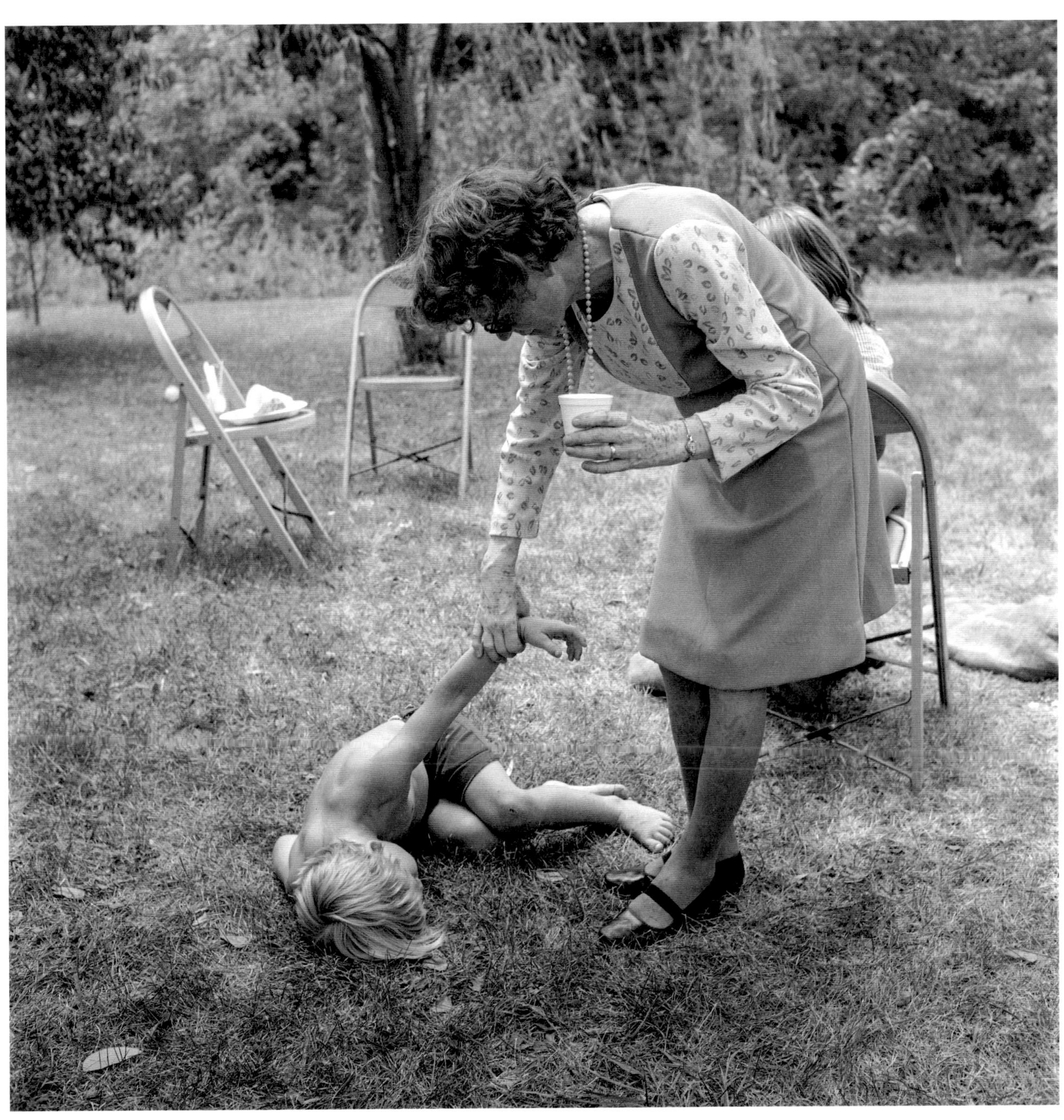

Jeff and Maggie, Danville, 1979

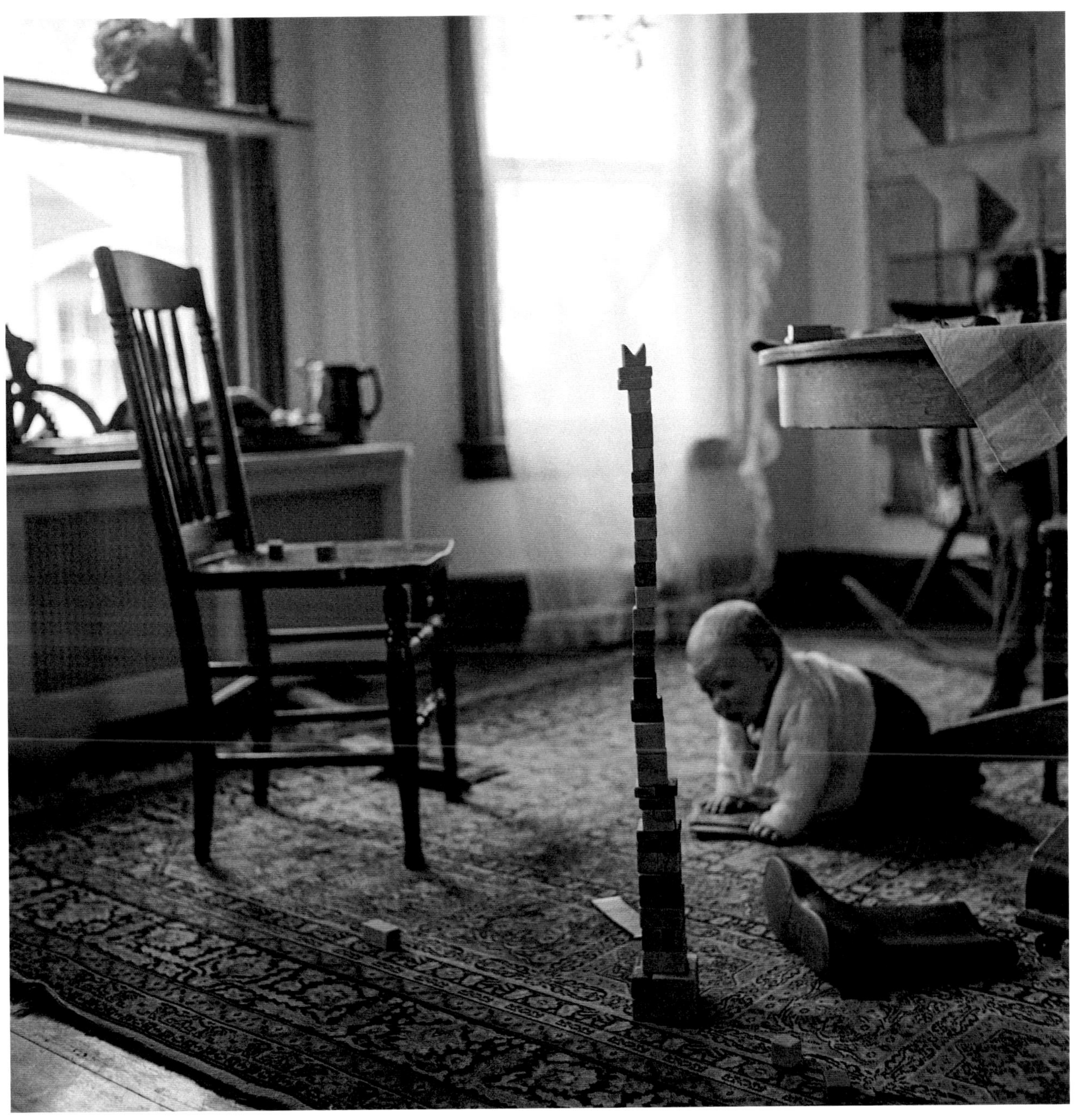

Isaac, Newtown, Pennsylvania, 1975

I'm aware of something as I go back and find images like this. I had made a kind of break with the tradition I started out in, the idea of the "decisive moment." I moved on from that in the sense that when I found an intriguing setting, I would say, "Edith, come and stand in the middle of this, because we need a person here for reference. You have to stand for humanity." But the pictures I'm going back and finding now didn't happen that way. I would see the children doing something, and I would think, how elegant and exotic, and how driven by their own body wisdom. They'd turn the act of being in a chair into a creative activity. One foot finds the doorknob, the other foot finds the knee. And all these combinations are just being channeled by their innate, unconscious self. They're not self-conscious at all. I know I valued that, but it wasn't what I was thinking. If I thought of myself as doing something new, the "new thing" wouldn't have been pictures like this. Maybe that's why I overlooked them for such a long time.

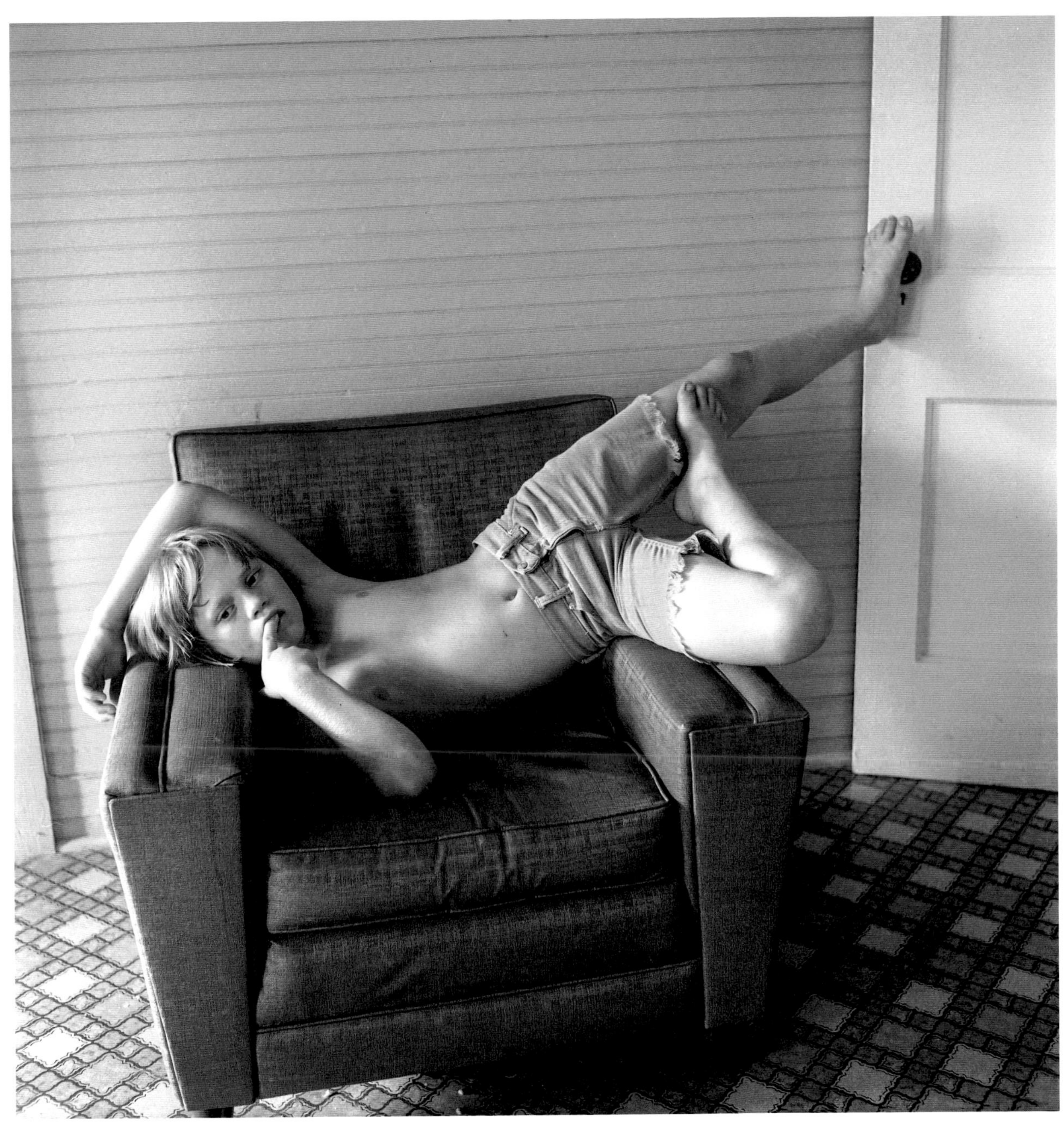

Dwayne, Danville, 1974

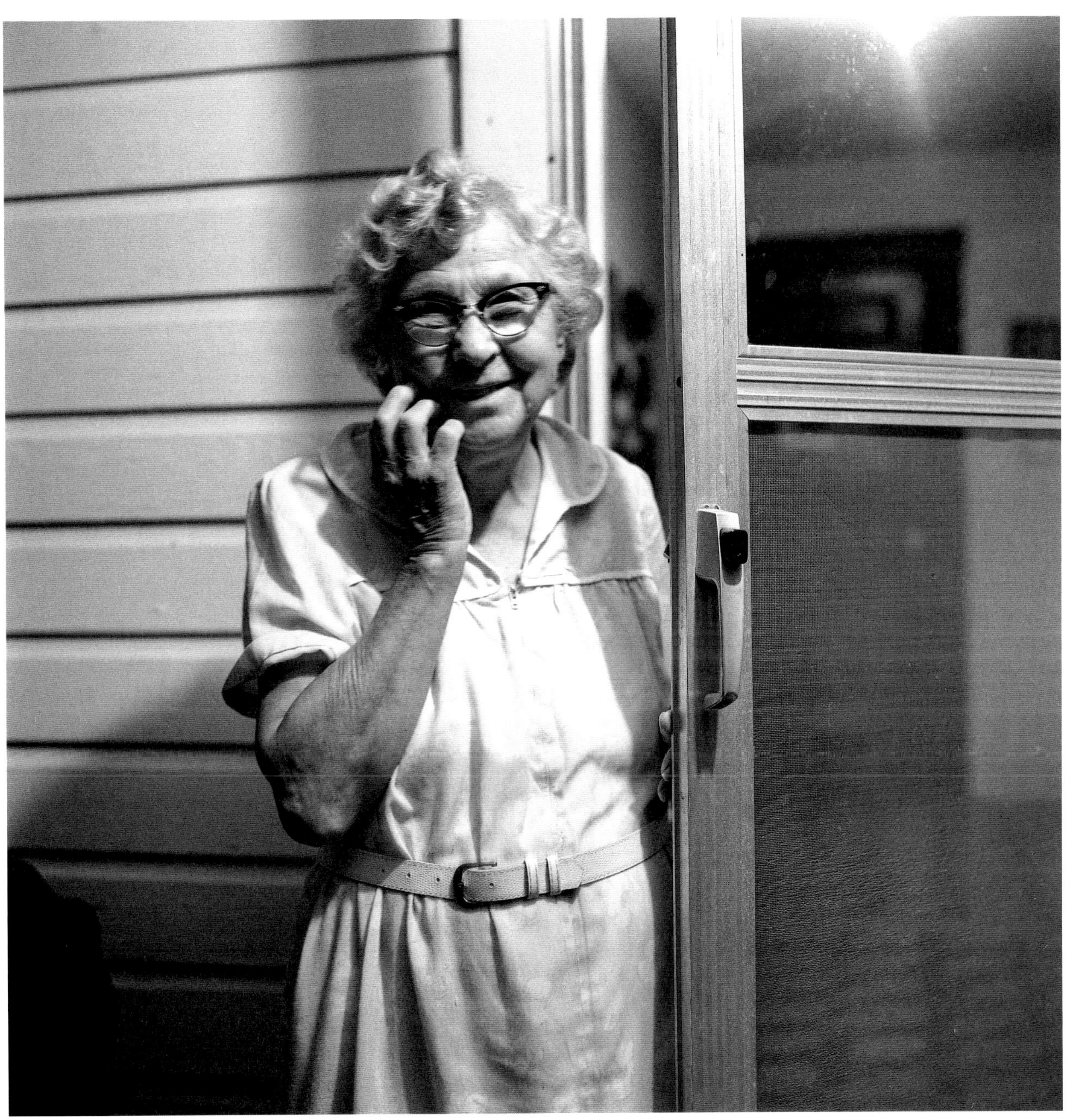

Gertrude Mitchell, Danville, 1992

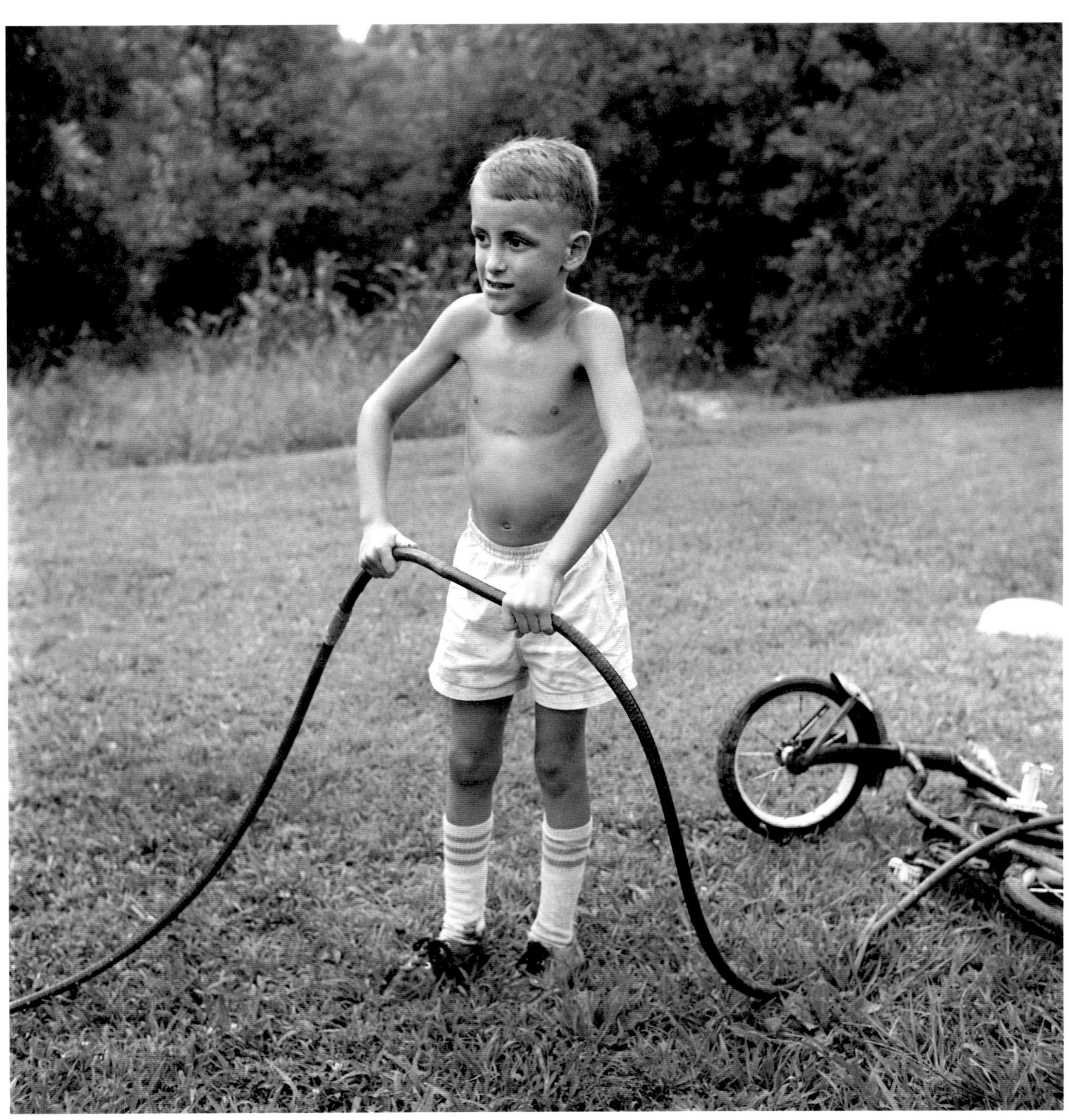

Ready to stop the Water, Danville, 1979

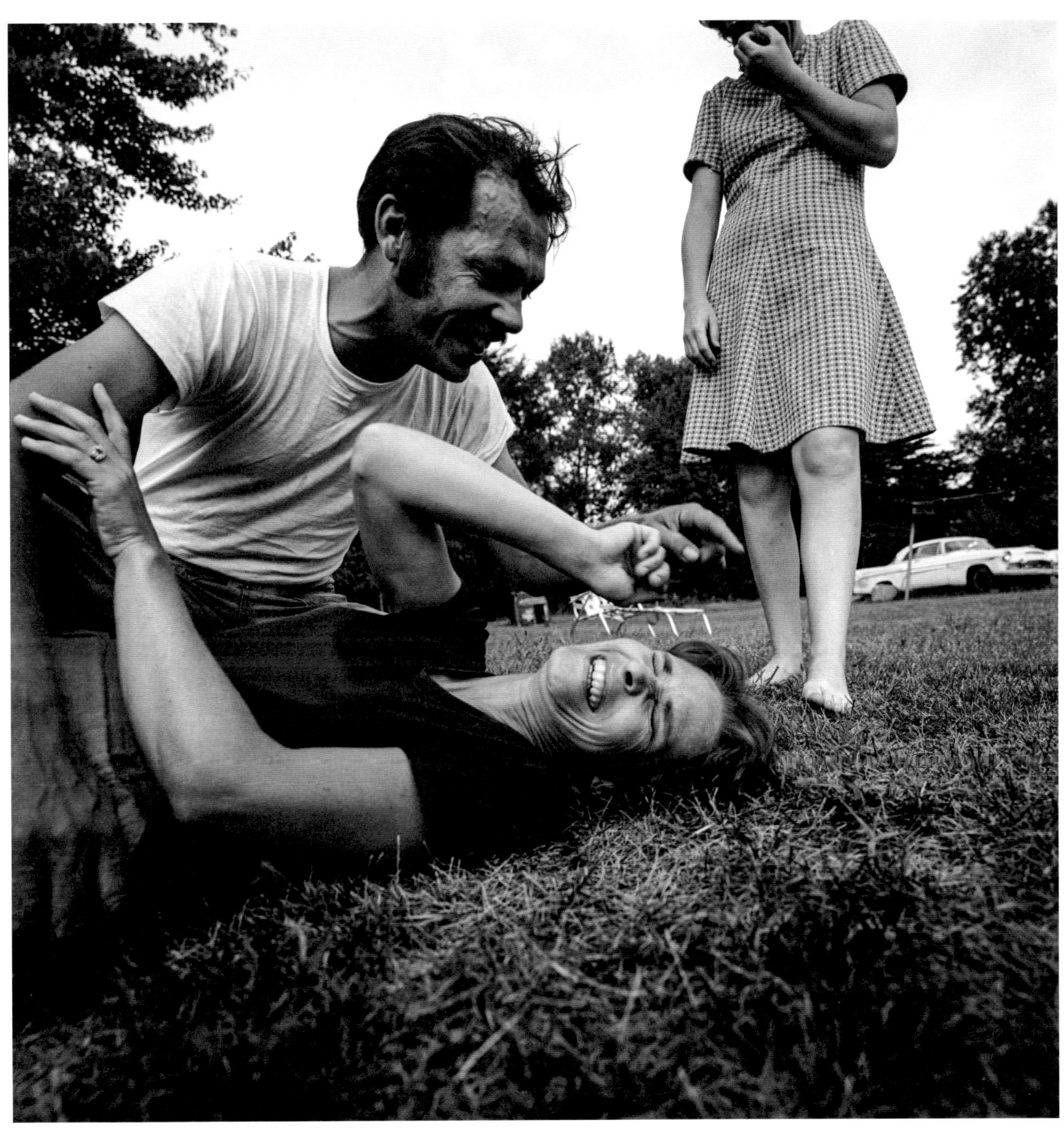

David and Mae, with Helen, Danville, 1976

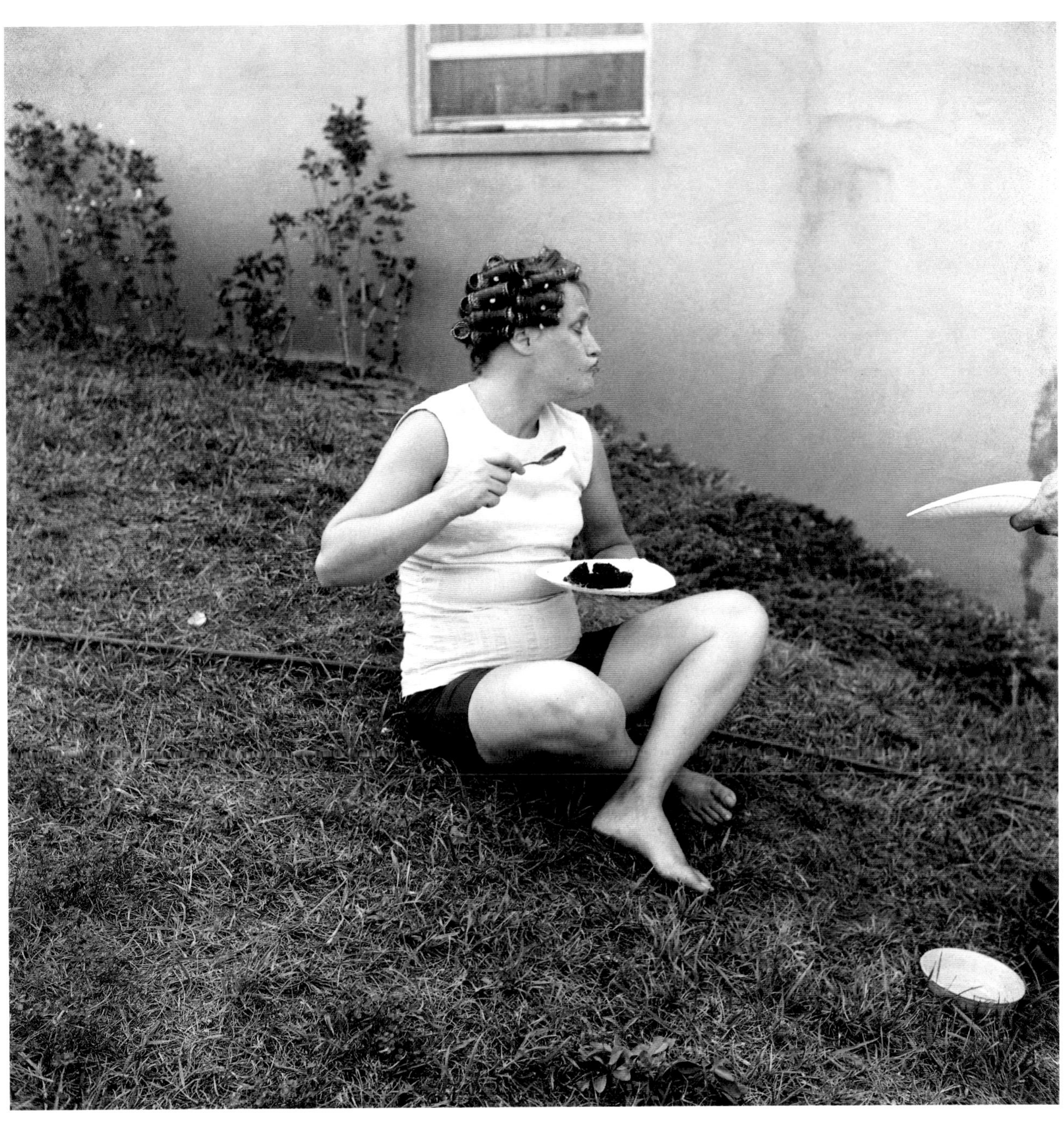

Ruth, Chatham, Virginia, 1979

I love the way the family farm is only implied: the woodpile, the distant pasture, and something seedy about it that feels eternal. You could have seen that same scene a hundred years earlier. When my grandfather Elijah's uncle Allen came to his last day of service in the Confederate Army, he happened to be at Appomattox Court House, in Virginia, when General Lee surrendered. After the surrender, he walked home. I think it was less than ten miles.

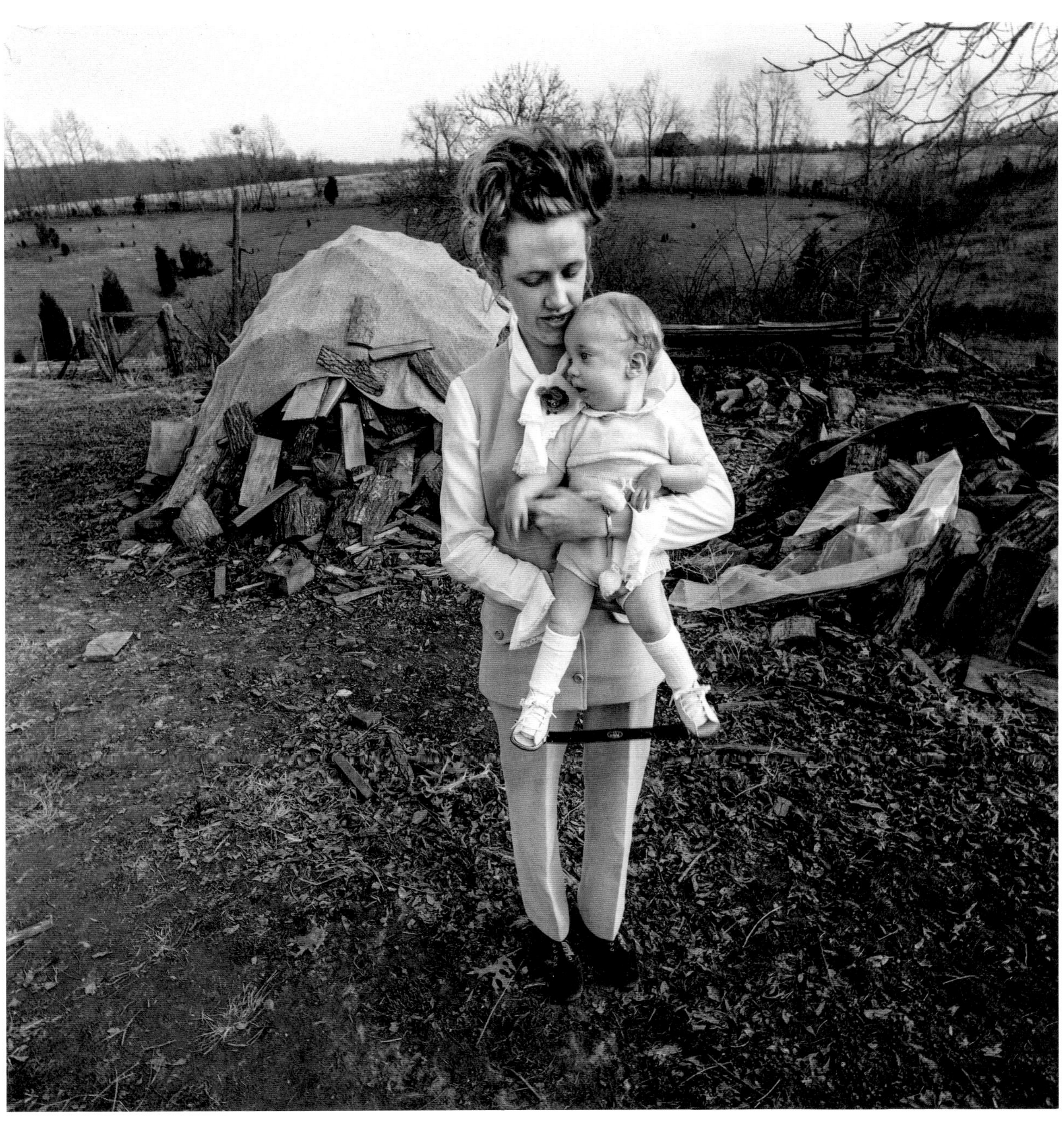

Buckingham County, Virginia, 1972

Reva would go off and buy a fancy chair once in a while, on time. It was not real leather.

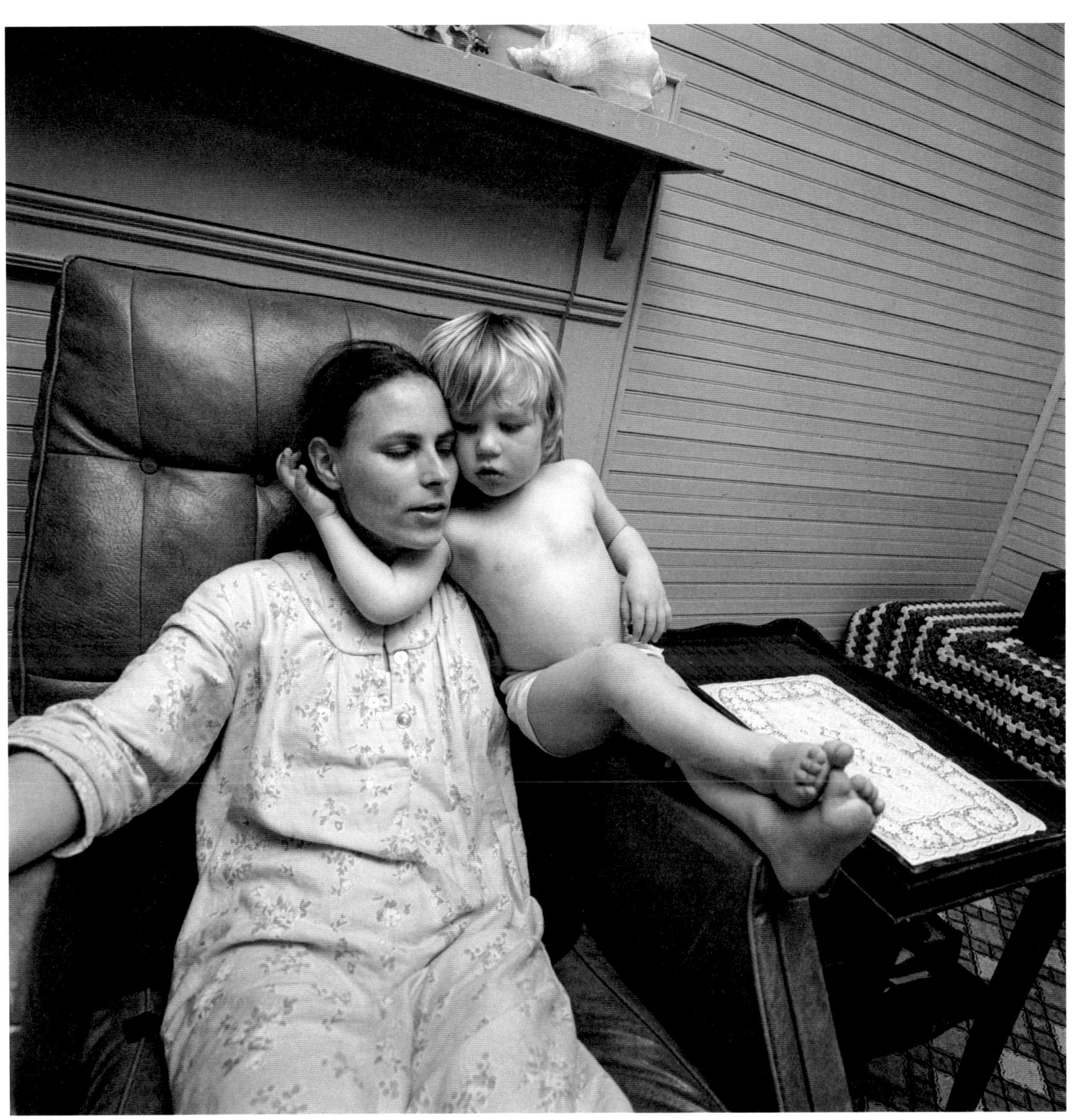

Edith and Isaac, Danville, 1978

You wouldn't know what he was collecting, but it's meaningful to me, because now I find myself with my own fig tree, and I'm older than he was.

EDITH *Look how delicately he's holding that basket.*

From a letter to Italian friends, dated 1976:

"At least for the moment. And it is a dream to smile at, run through by the cold deep water flow of recognition: I am my father's son. And age itself and fragileness has made father more available to me. I photographed him this August under his fig tree as he collected fruit.

In the past two years he has lost his extra weight, almost forty pounds, and now is close to his weight of high school days. The bones of his face more clearly reveal my source and I can see myself near to death in him and in Isaac I see my face too, beyond memory."

That's probably in his last year or two. Mother had just died. It totally humanized him, in the most beautiful way. It pulled the rug from under him, too, when he did not have her stability and her moral clarity.

EDITH *She was a much more gentle person, a much more spiritual person. She always felt positive about everything and never said anything negative. It was always something hopeful. And he could be a little arrogant, not unlike his father.*

You've heard me say, I think, that a guy asked me, "Why are you the way you are?" And I surprised myself by saying, "Because I wanted to be like my mother." I was at least seventy by the time I said that, and I had never quite confronted the reality that I was unconsciously modeling myself after my mother, not my father. In a way, in my youth, I was in absentia as much as I could be. I think I just trusted women better than I trusted men.

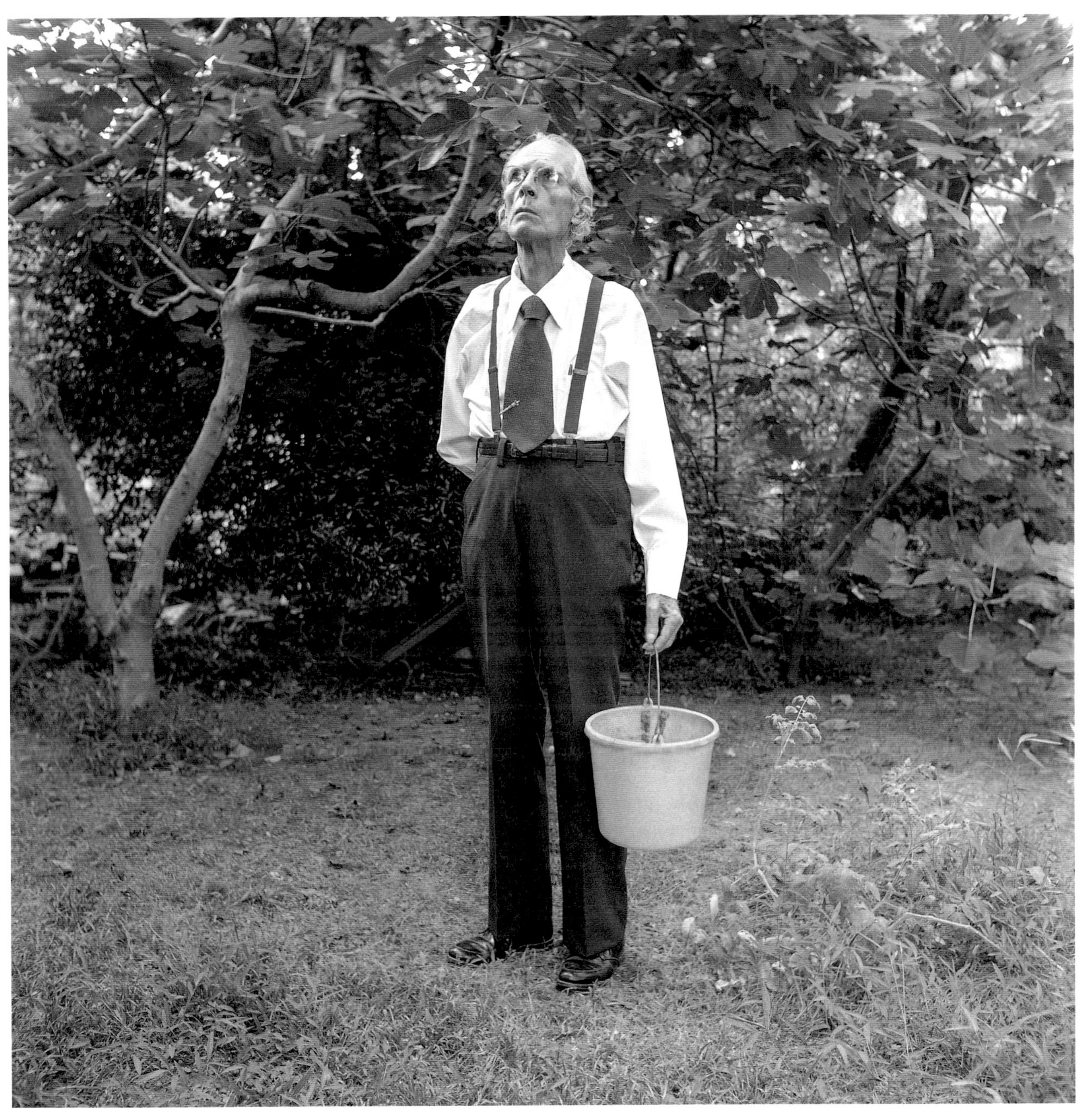

Collecting Figs, Pastor Gowin, Ocean View, Virginia, 1976

Two pastors and their wives at a family reunion. At least one of these pastors is related to Edith's mother.

EDITH *It's my grandmother's brother. I think one of them is her sister, and one is her brother. My grandmother grew up in Appalachia, near Bristol.*

We took Reva to a family reunion where she knew she would be seeing her mother's kin. I remember the day and the experience superwell, but I never saw this picture when I was young. I don't know what I would have thought about it then, but I absolutely adore it now. I just think it's unbelievable. The body language of the four individuals.

EDITH *We went up to their church, and they were singing shape note.*

The one on the right might be the one who played fiddle when he was young. I think we stopped at his house in Galax. Reva wanted him to play his violin, but he said, "No, Reva, I used to play the dances, but now that I got the Lord, I'm not playing my fiddle no more." I just thought that was all profound material. You change teams in the middle of the game. You switch over—like being from Brooklyn and going to the Yankees.

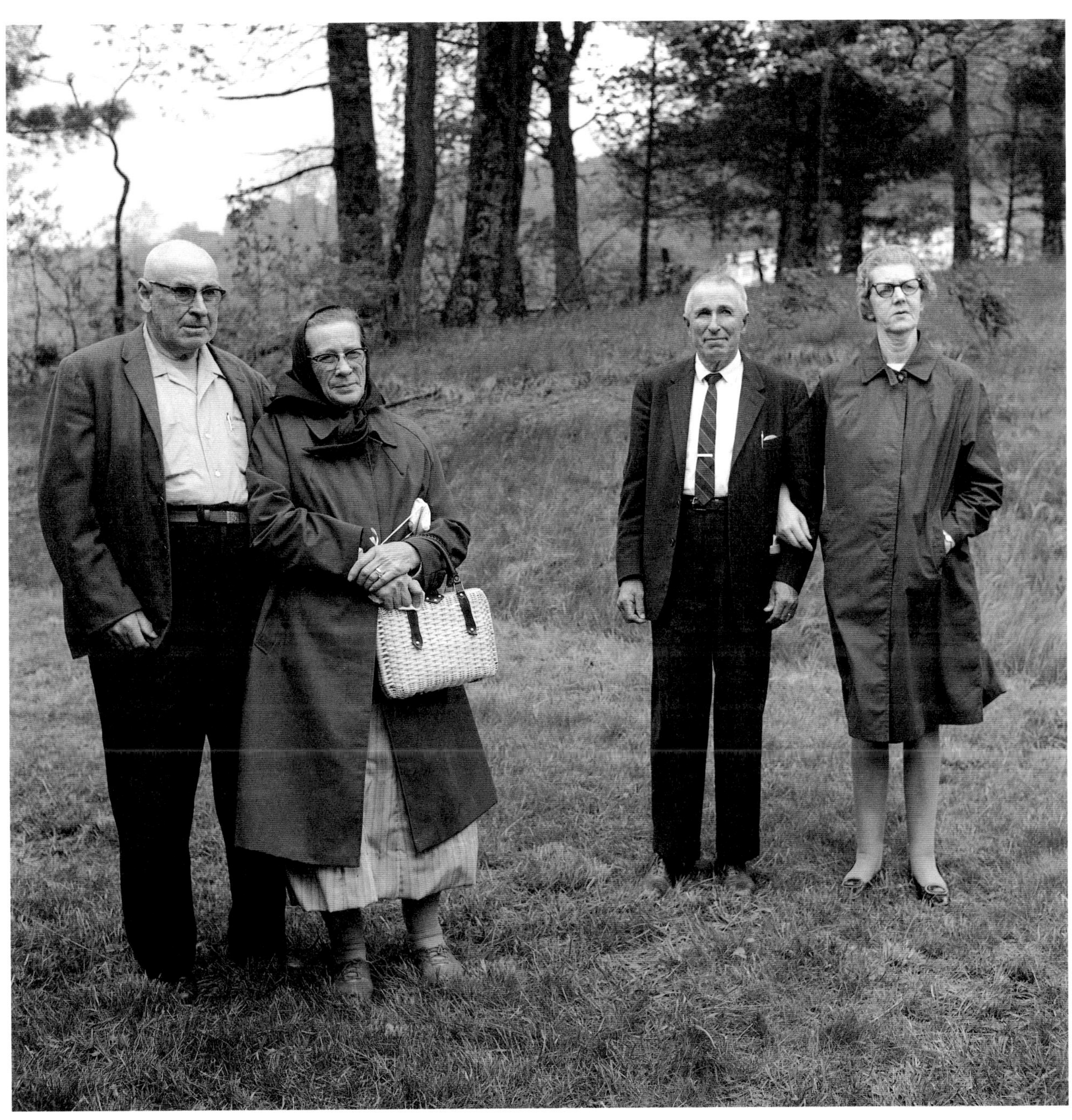

Two Pastors and Their Wives at a Family Reunion, near Galax, Virginia, 1970

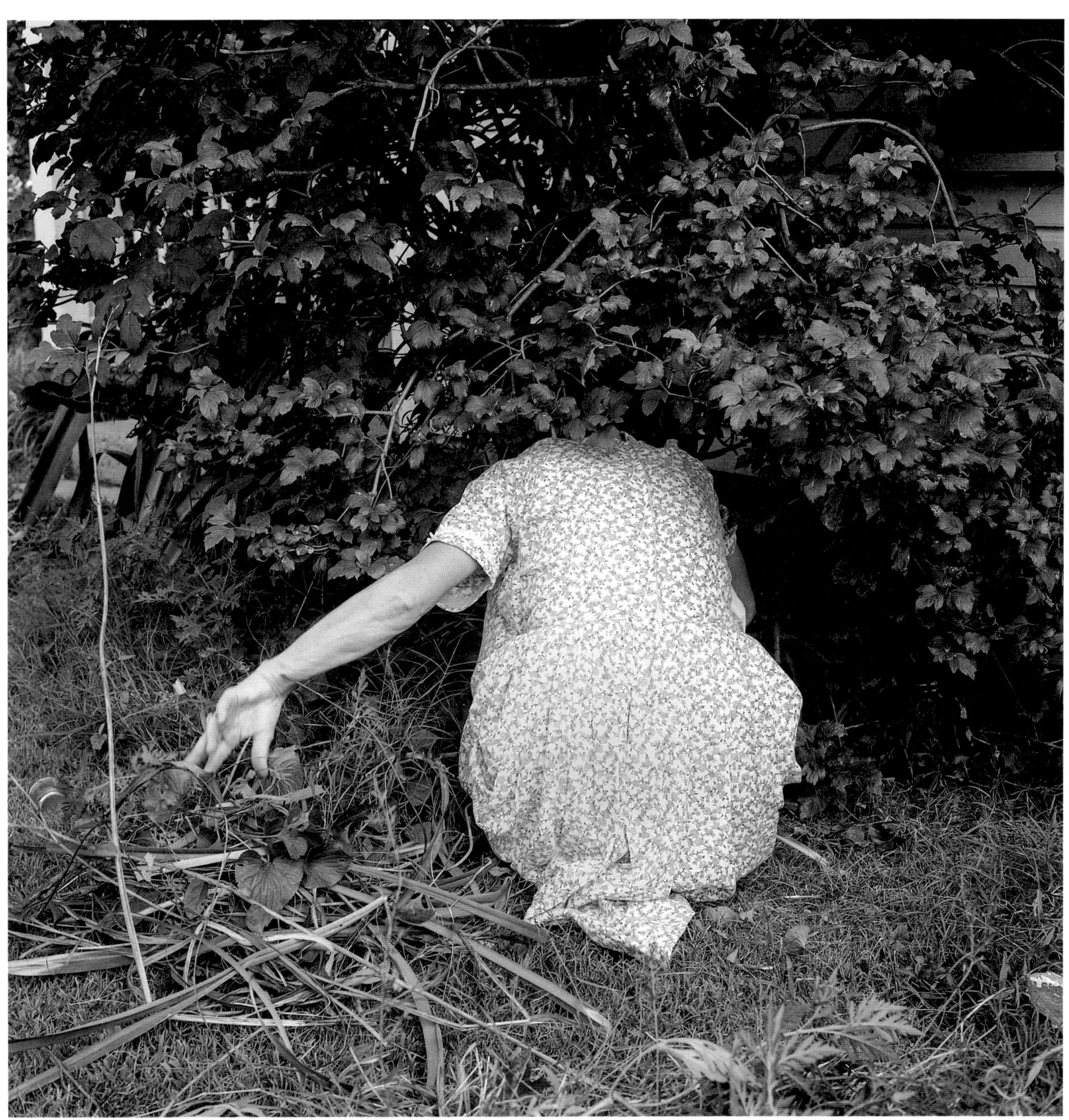

Reva Weeding, Danville, 1974

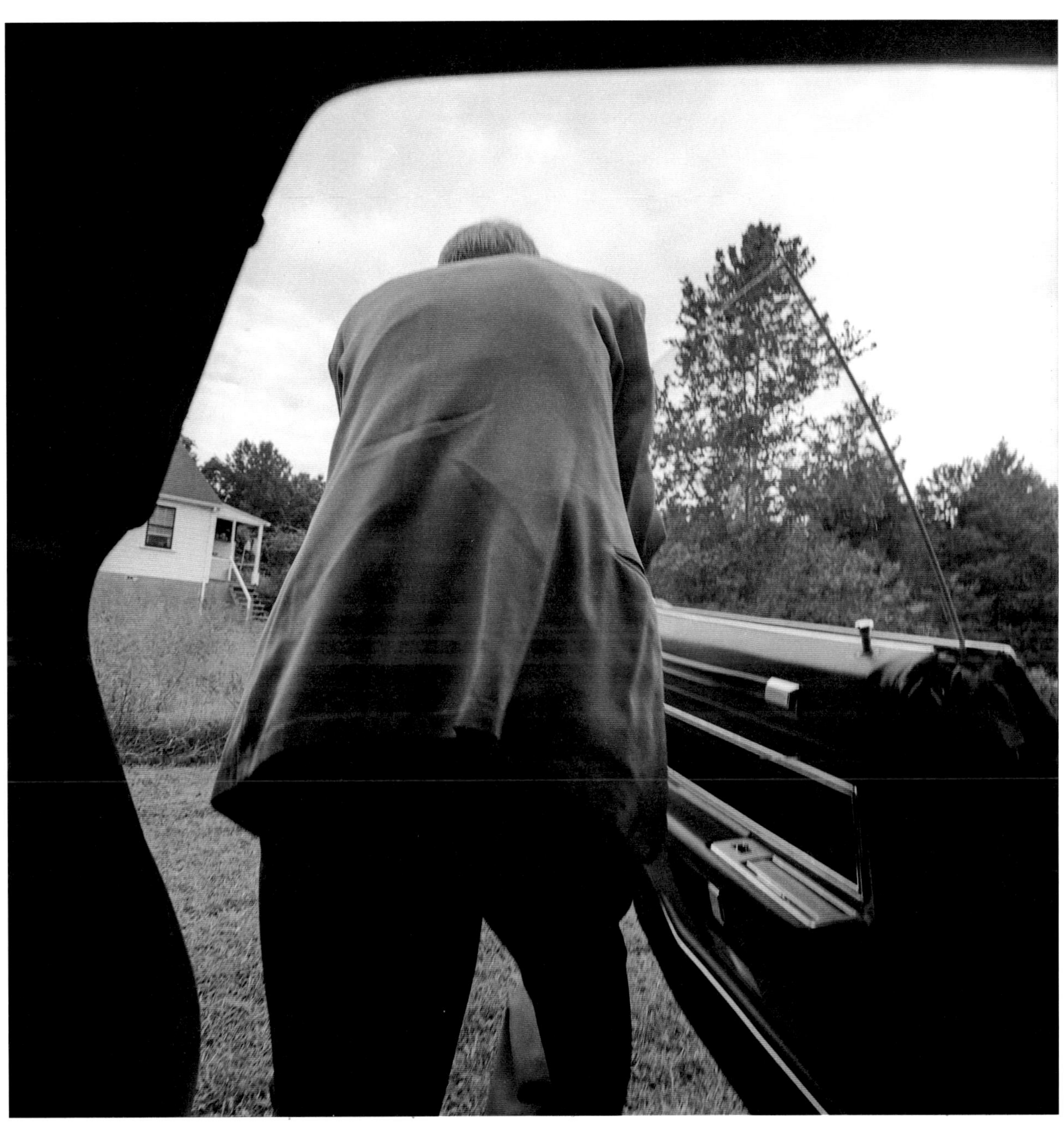

Raymond, Danville, 1972

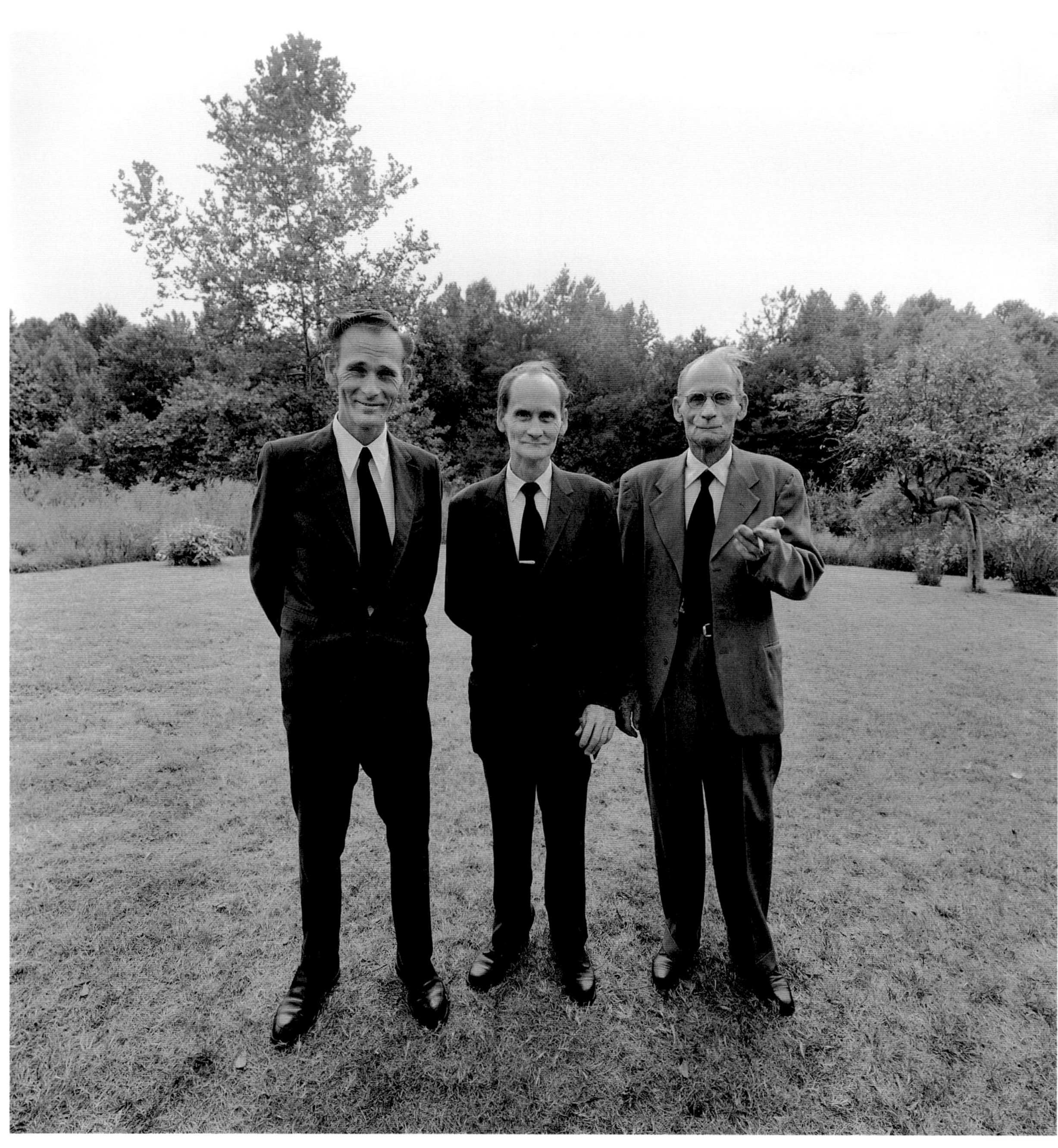

Popeye, Ralph, and Raymond, Danville, 1972

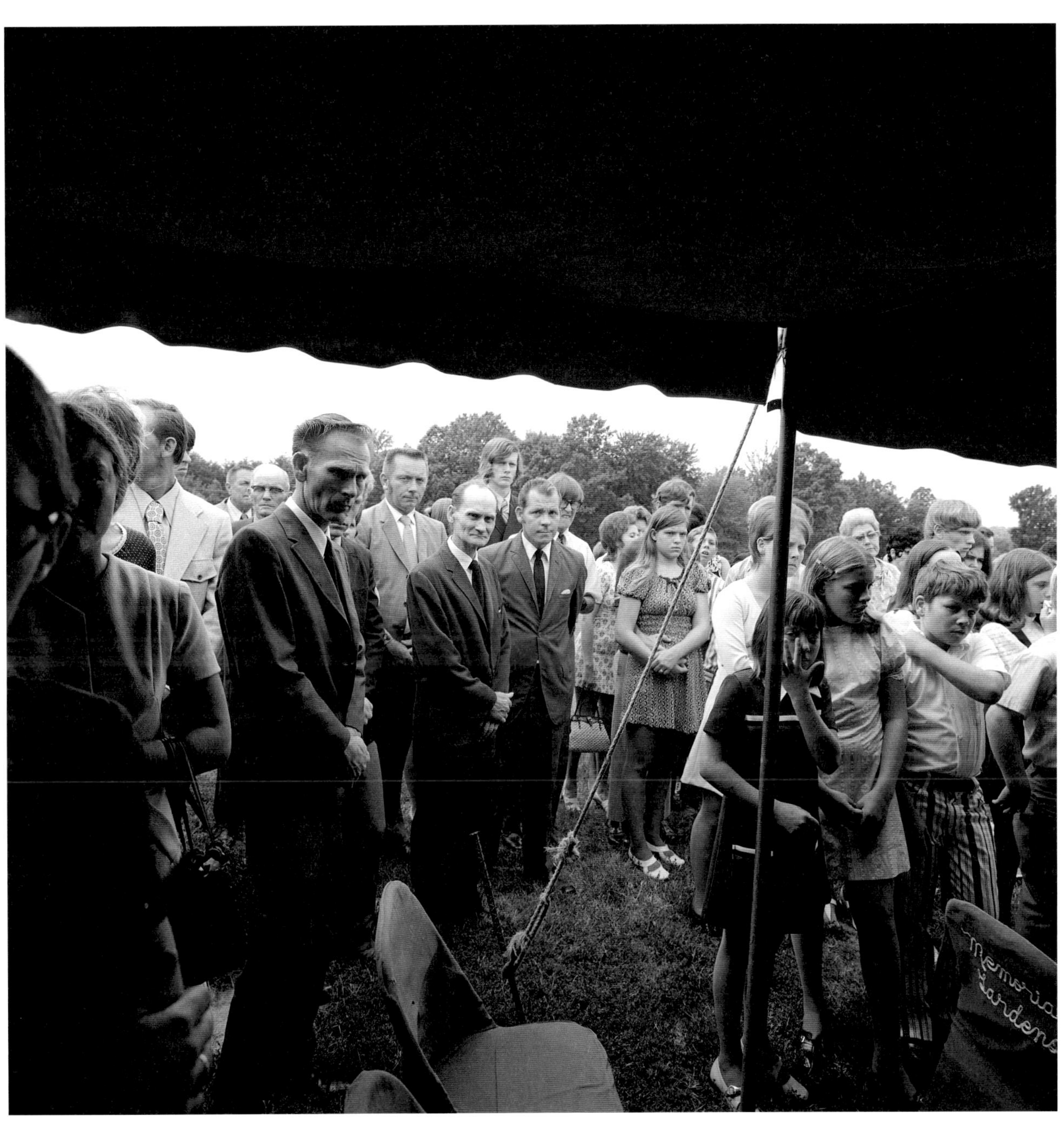

At Rennie Booher's Funeral, Danville, 1972

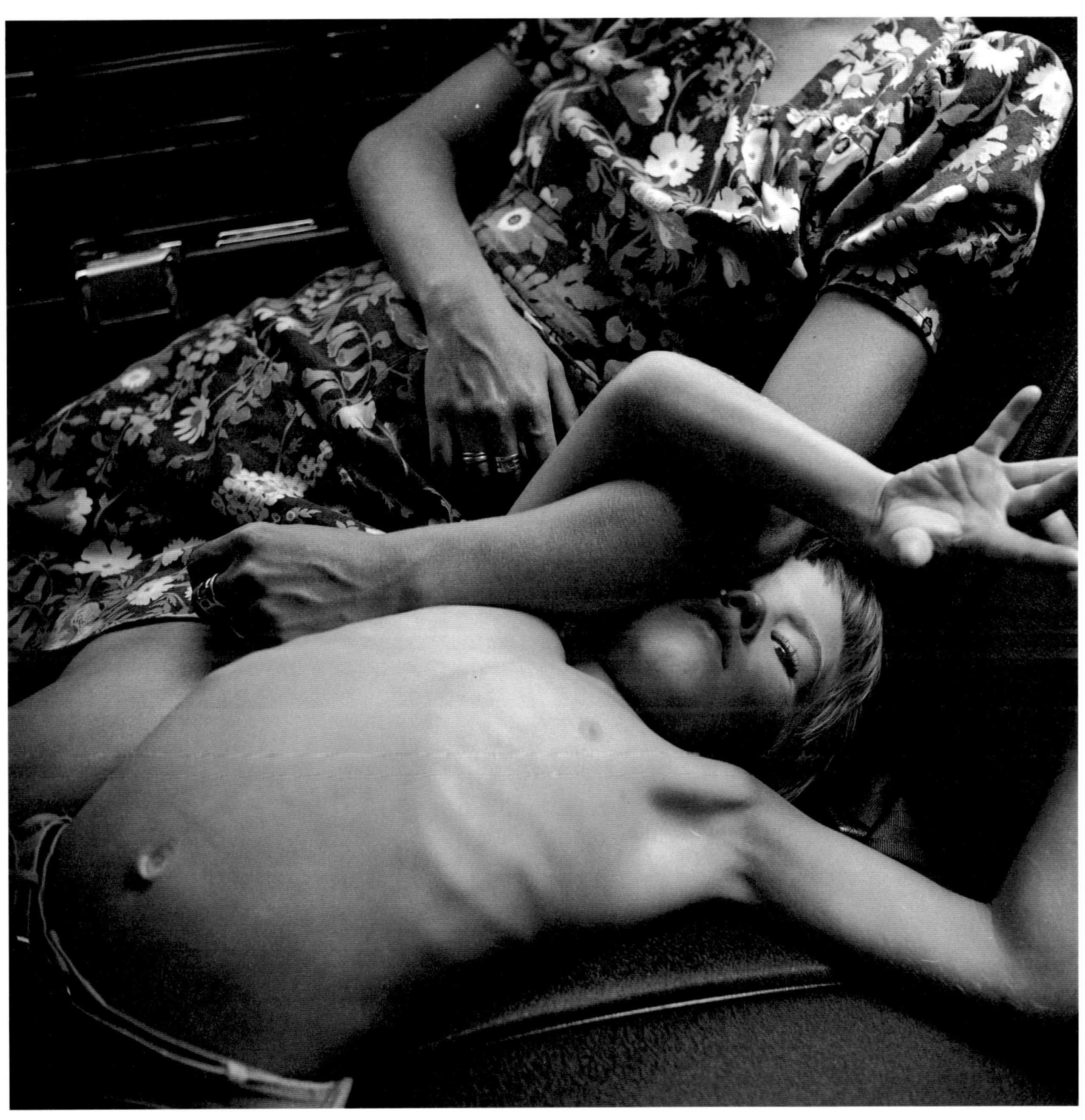

Edith and Elijah, Danville, 1972

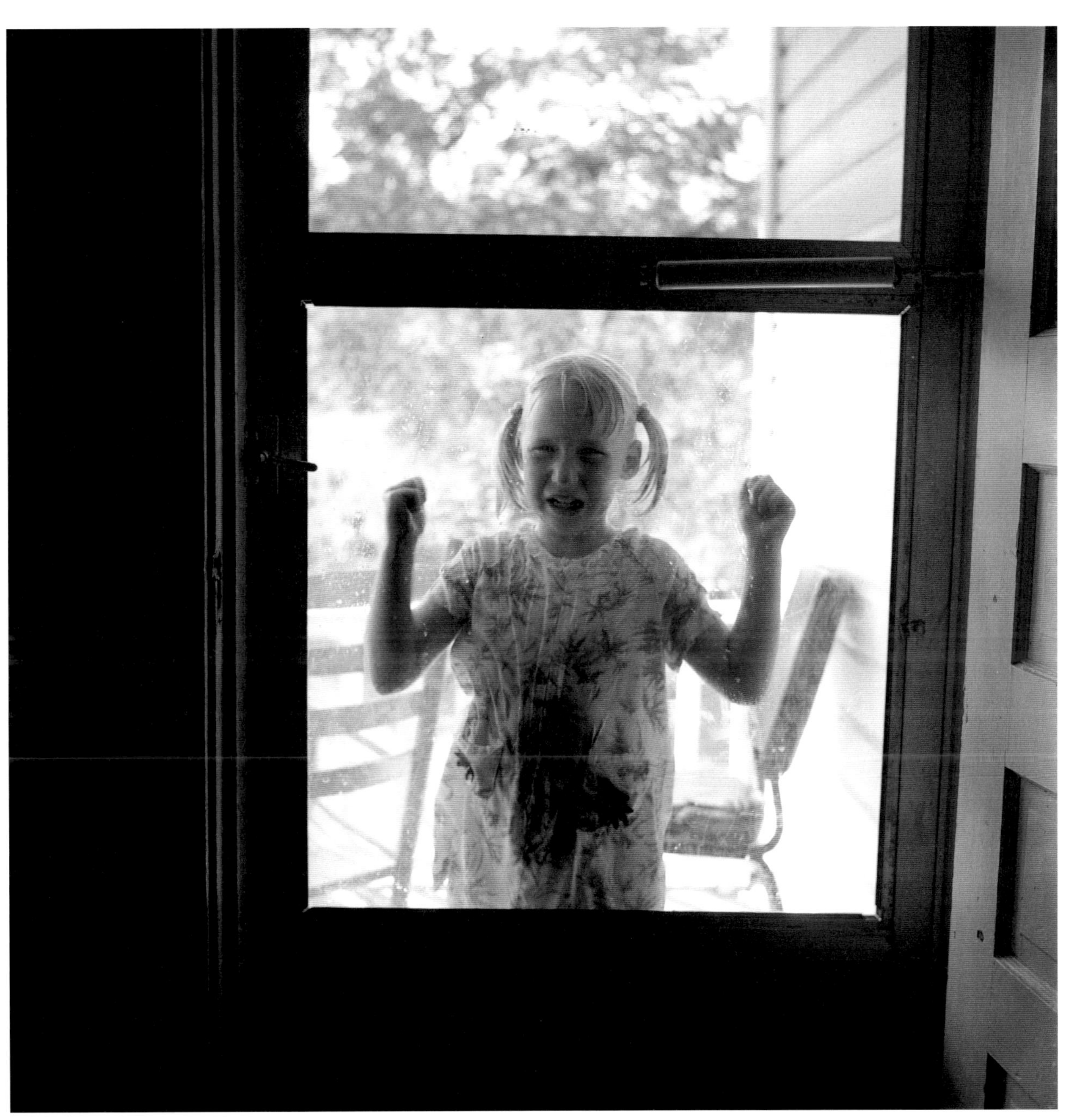

Amy, Danville, 1975

Then I probably only saw her face, her hands. Now I also love the handles of the refrigerator, the aluminum trim, the race car, the little stuff. It was on a day like this that we showed Maggie and Willie the Diane Arbus book the first time. They found it really interesting. Almost nothing was said about it, but they studied it like it was a profound introduction to a world they had not seen before but that they understood, in a way: they knew it was there. I don't think they ever thought they were in those pictures in any way. Nor did I. But I did understand that what I was interested in and what Arbus was interested in had a great deal in common. When we saw Arbus's photographs the first time, we thought, oh, well, we're almost doing that. We're making those pictures. Sort of. Only it's us. It was very affirming. But I saw there was a difference, too.

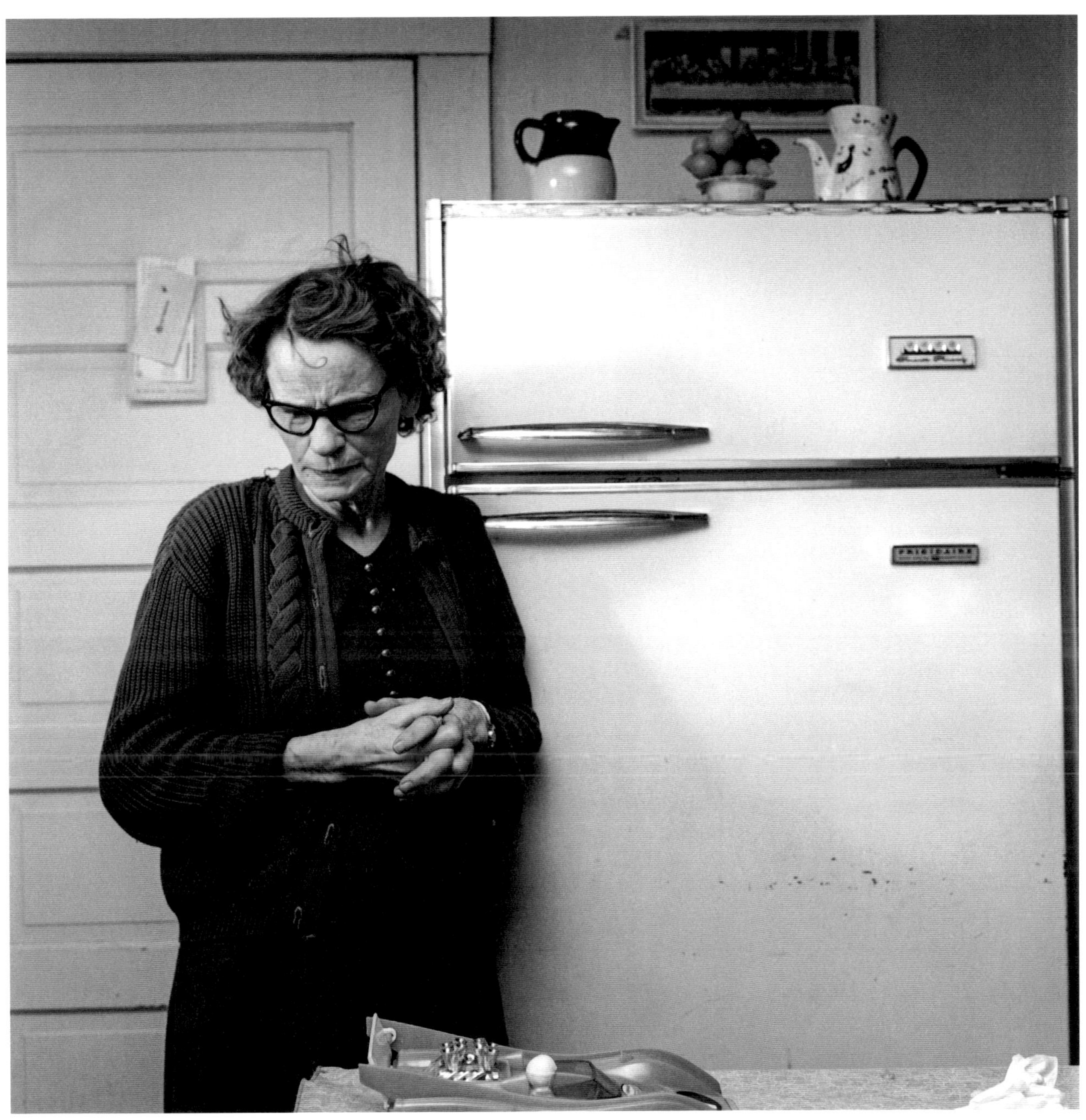

Maggie in Her Kitchen, Danville, 1975

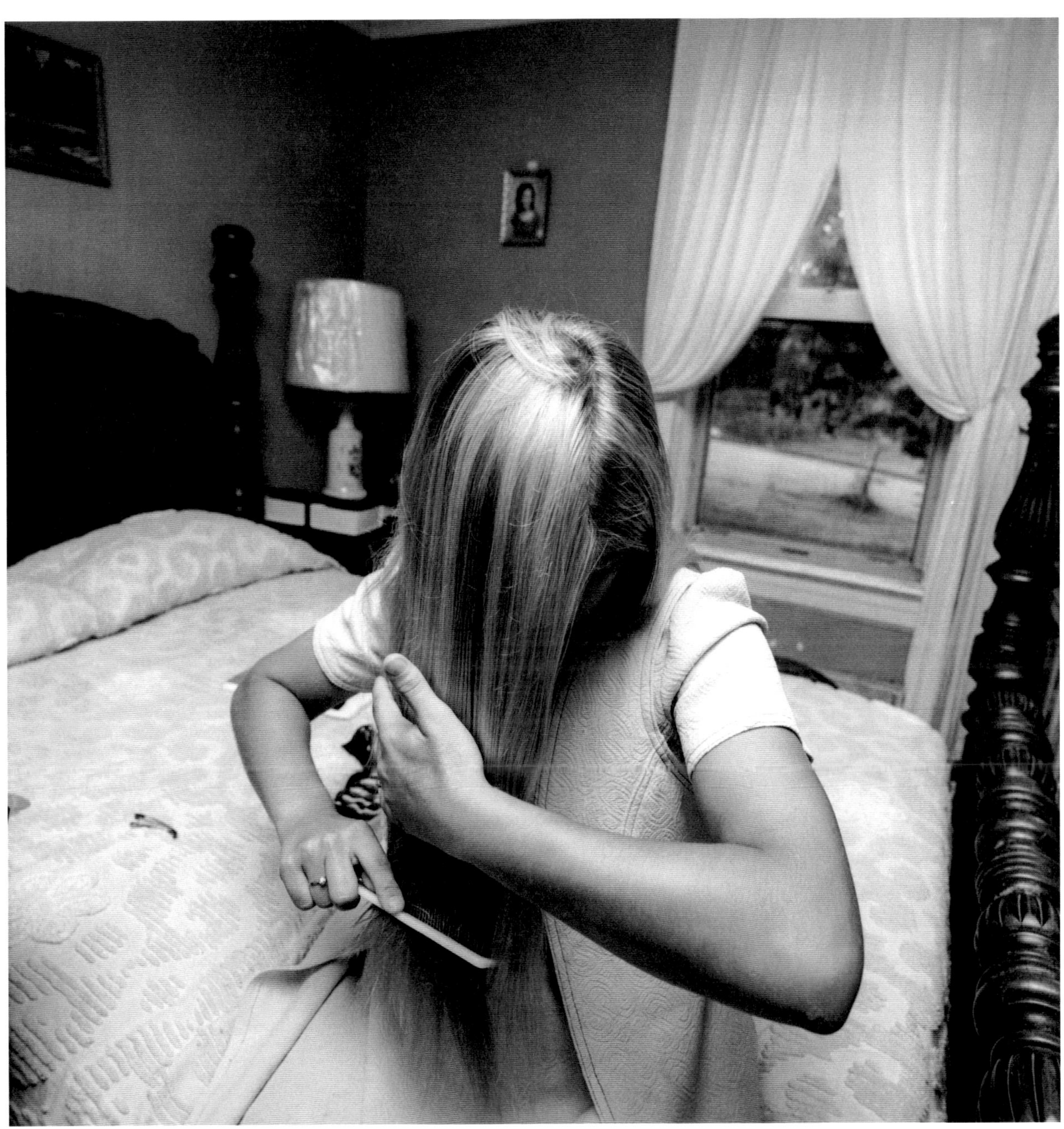

Darlene, Danville, 1974

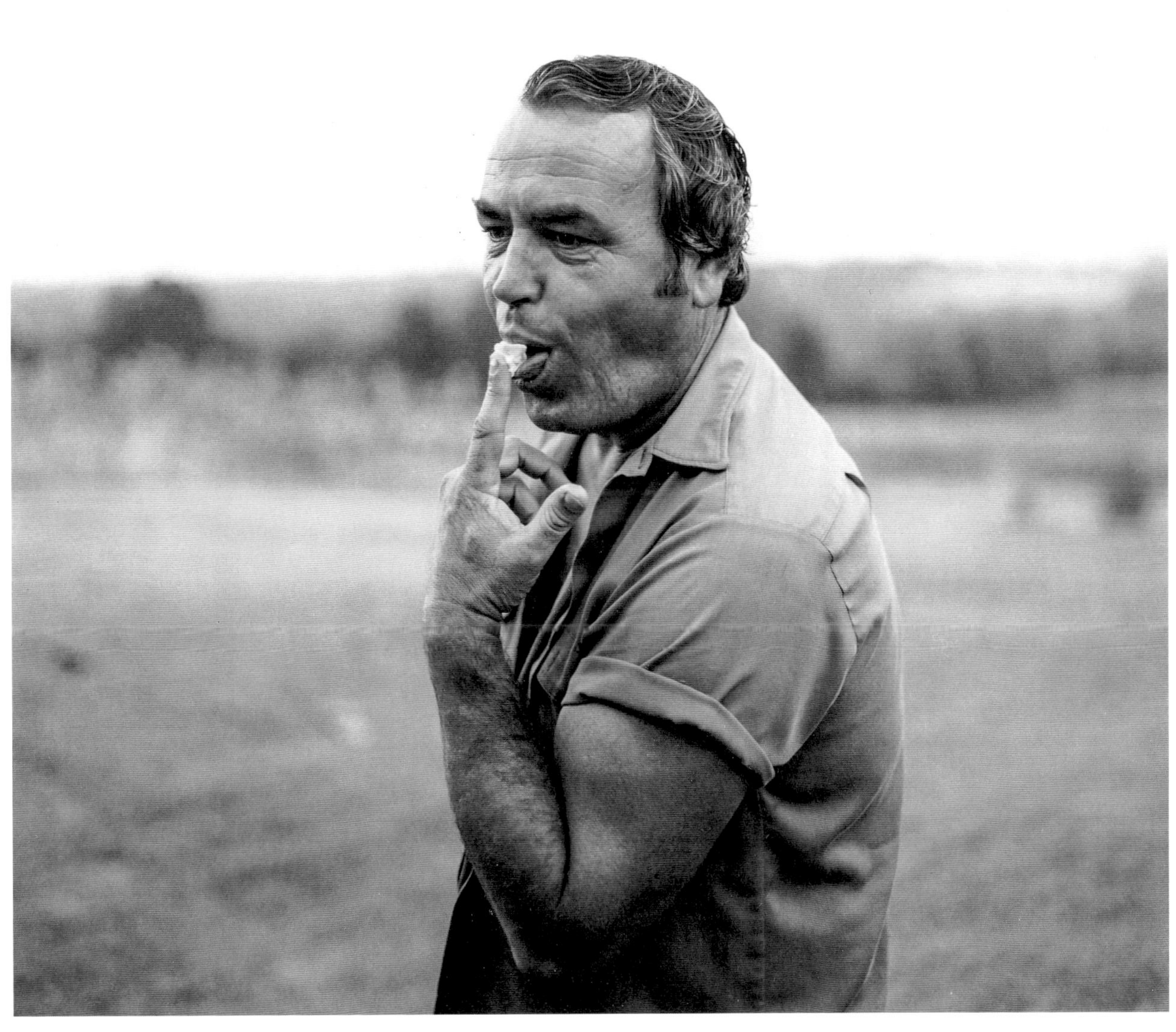

Luther, Chatham, Virginia, 1981

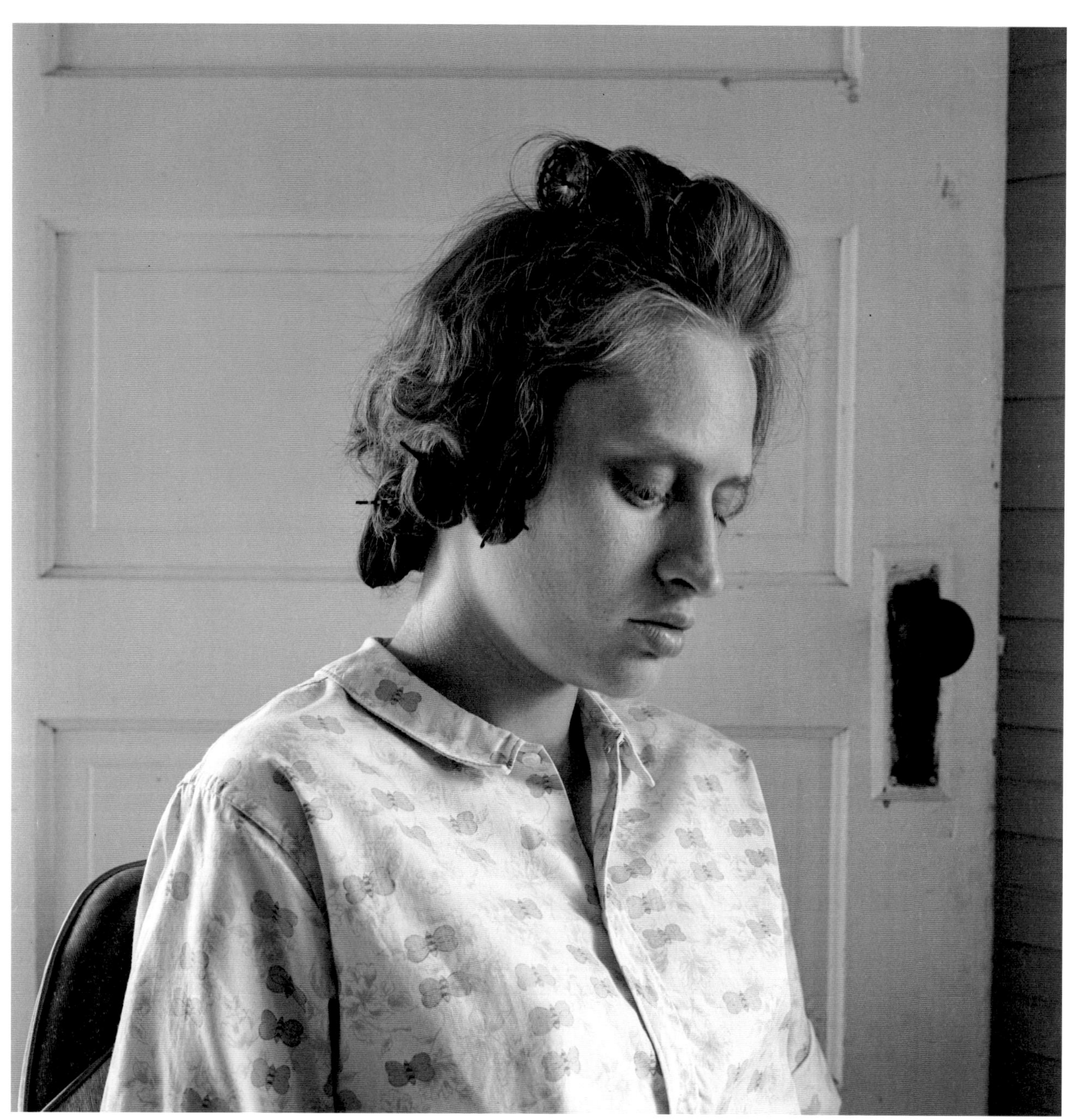

Ruth, Danville, 1967

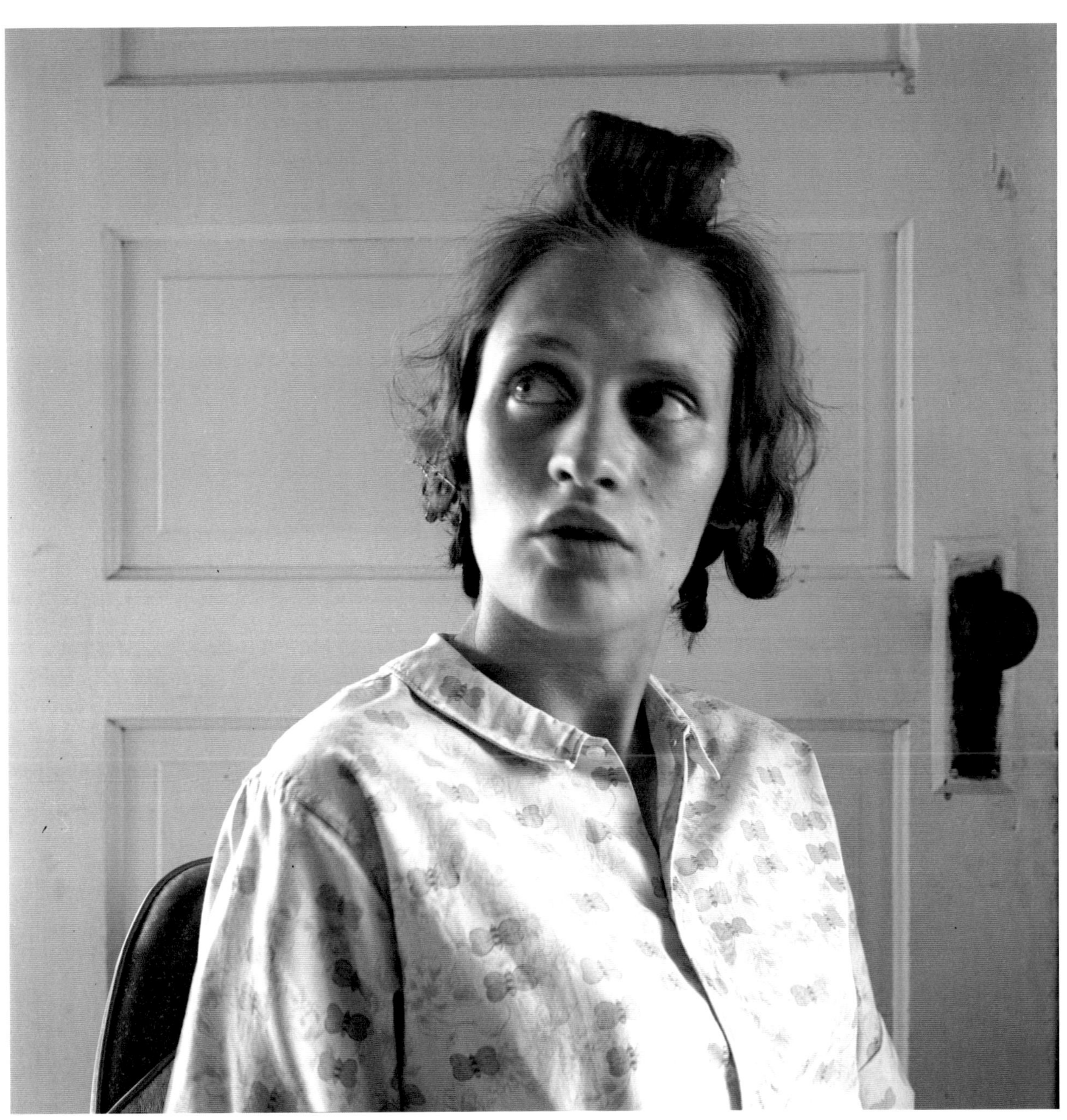

Ruth, Danville, 1967

Salt is the important ingredient here. I don't even remember taking the picture. I'm sure that I held off printing it because it reeked of symbolism. But it's right in the flow of images on that roll of film, the way life itself unfolds. Now I see in it the beauty of "the thing itself," and the joy of small things worthy of admiration and respect.

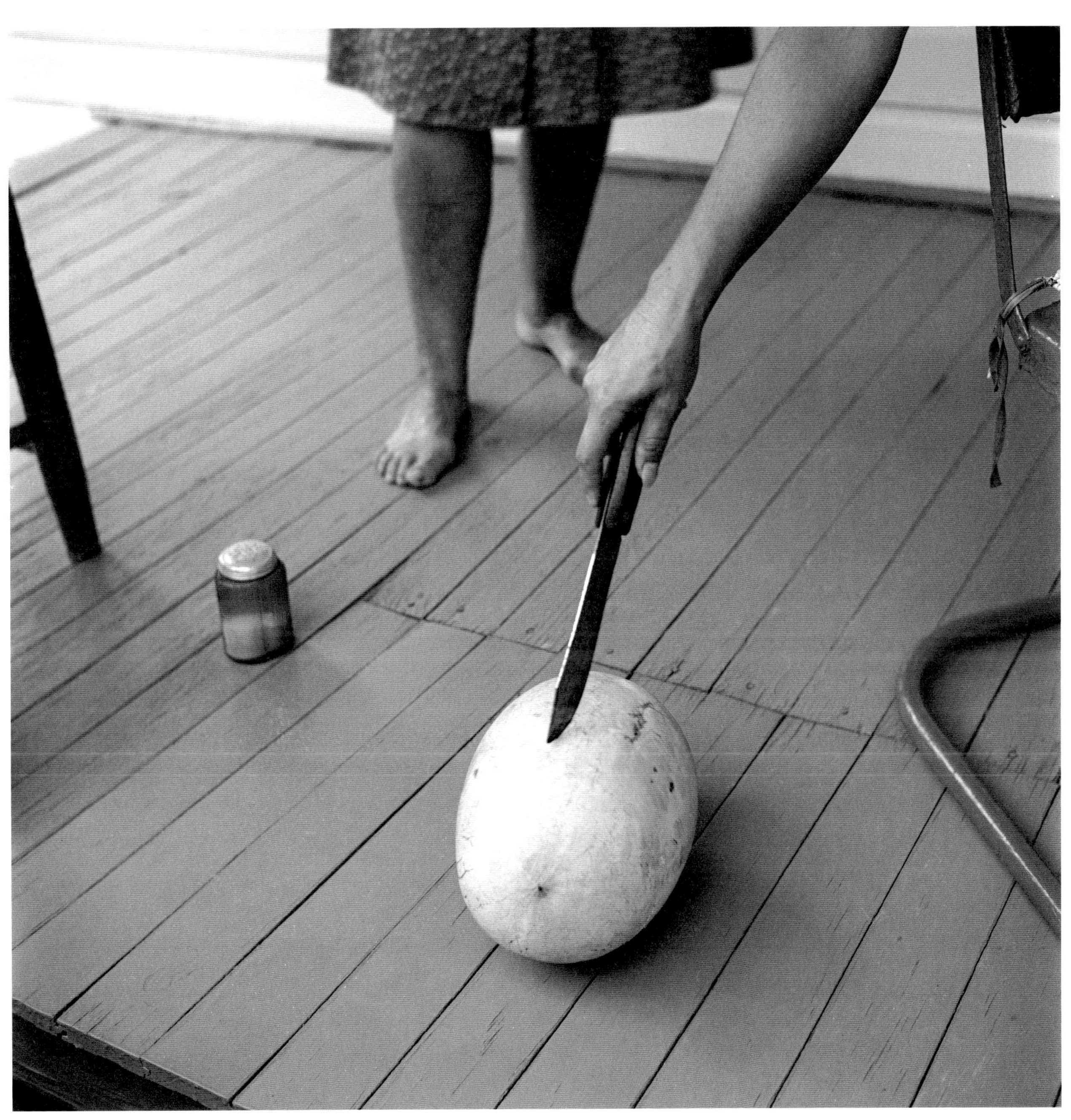

Gertrude's Melon, Danville, 1982

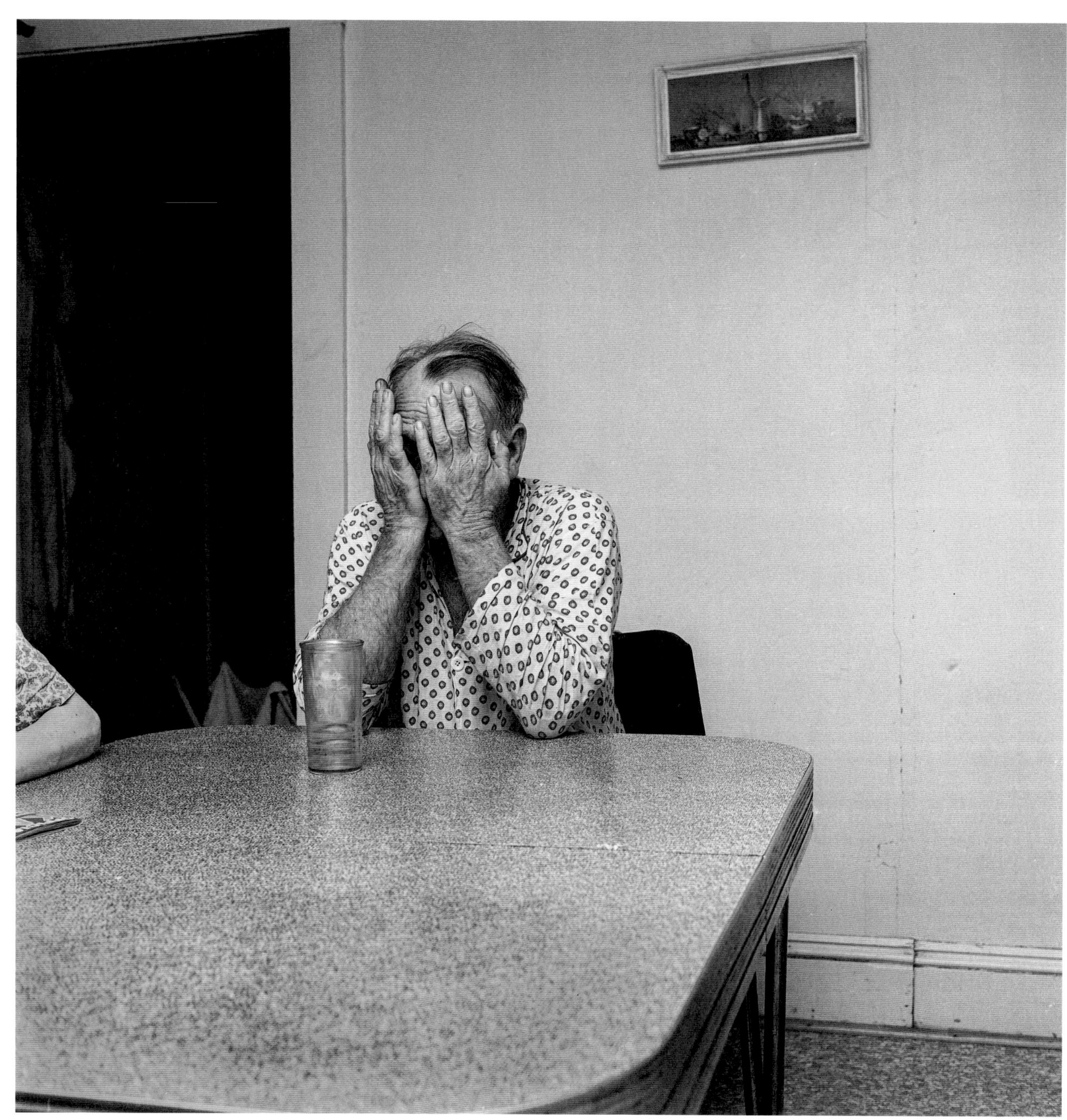

Willie Cooper, Danville, 1971

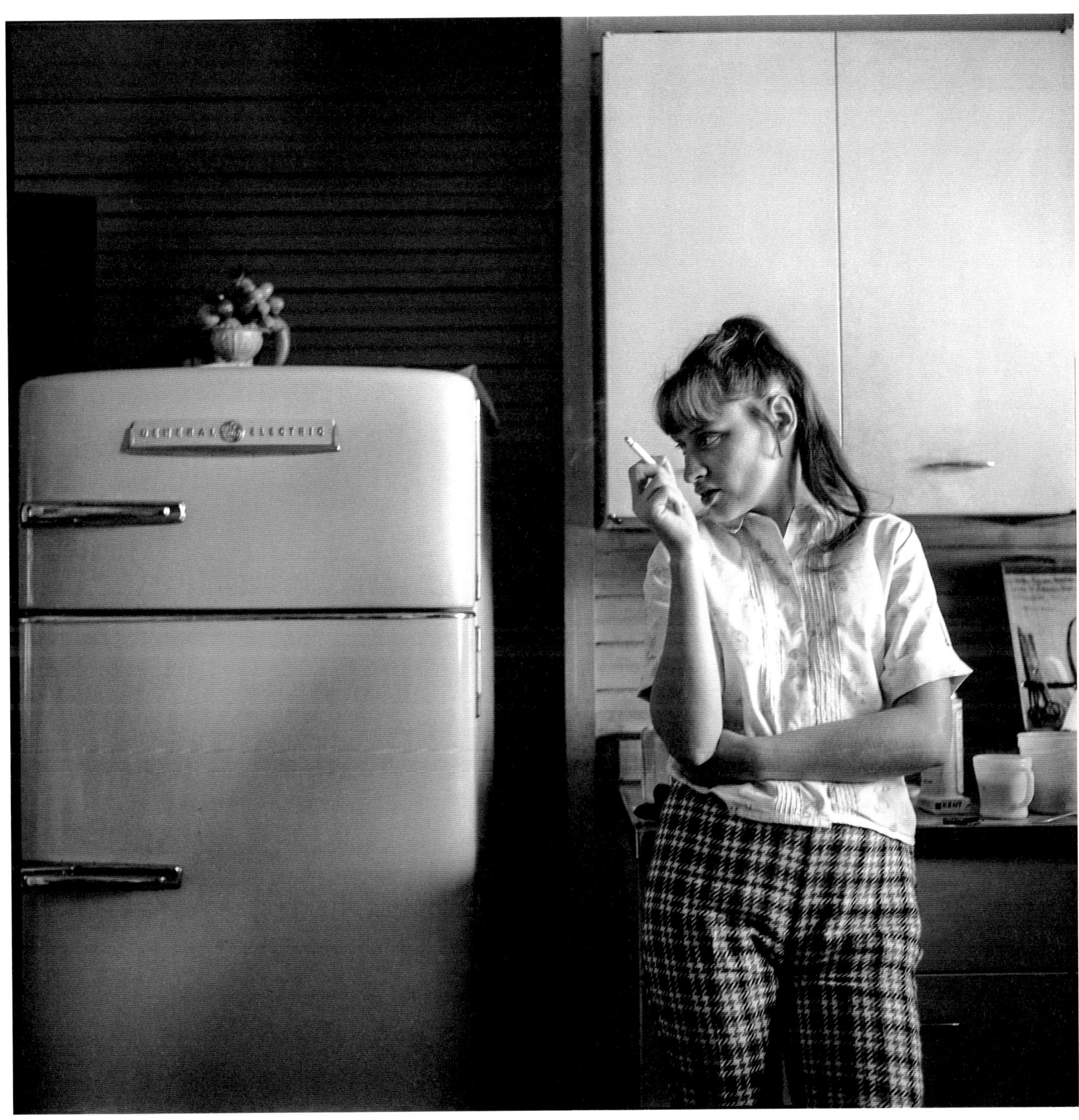

Ruth in Her Mother's Kitchen, Danville, 1968

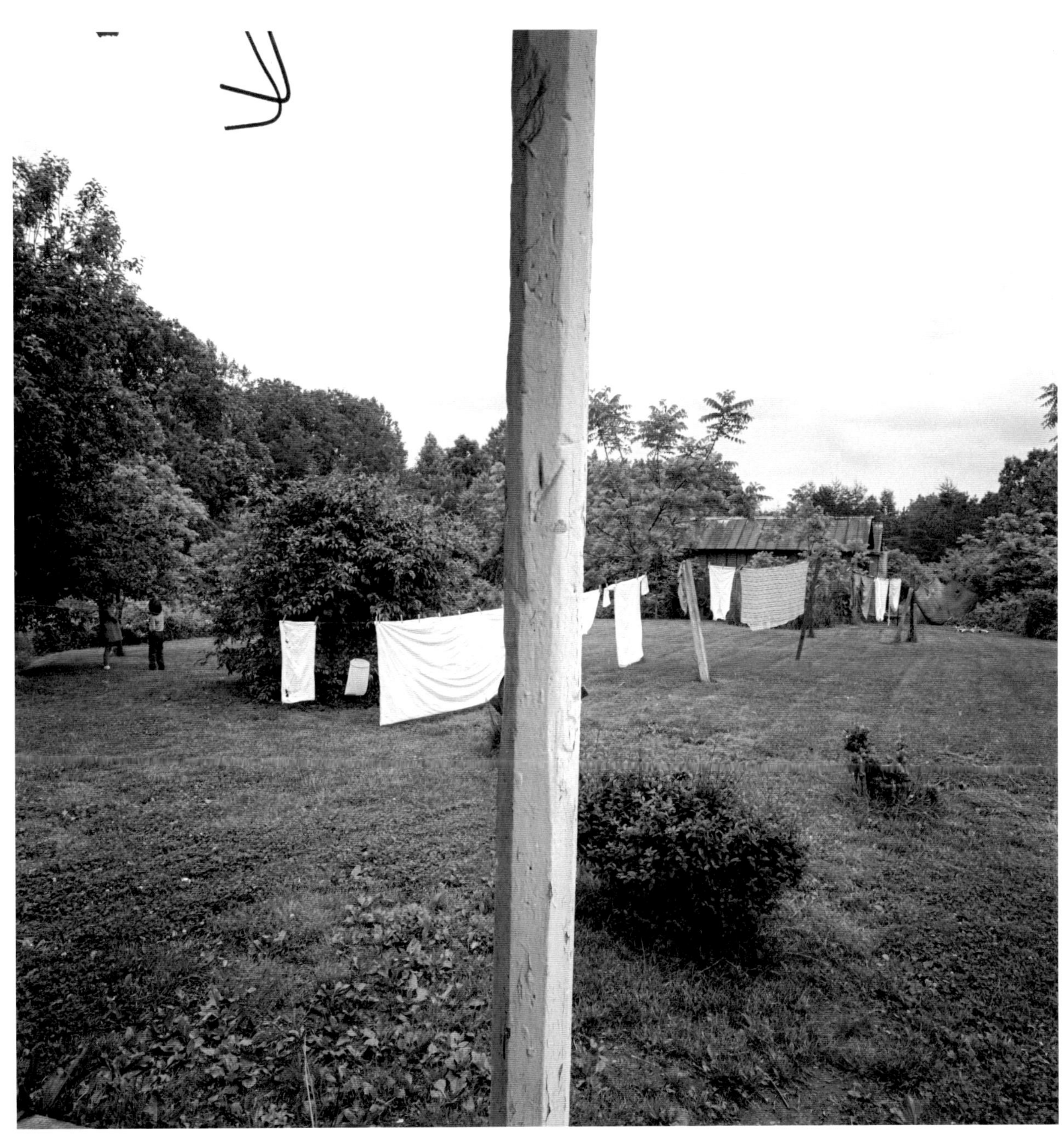

1916 Hand-Hewn Porch Post, Danville, 1972

The stand, there beside the television, is for a Victor photo lamp. By 1970, '71, I would take home 500-watt bulbs. And sometimes I would put a 250-watt bulb in a table lamp. It would be covered by a shade, so you didn't know, but it would amplify the light in the room so you could get a better luminosity. And not so long after that I started using flash as bounce. I might have had a flash then, but I don't think so. I think that was the problem. Even with those bulbs, with the 8×10, it was still a one-second exposure. That's a long time if anything's happening. And you still need all the light just to illuminate enough.

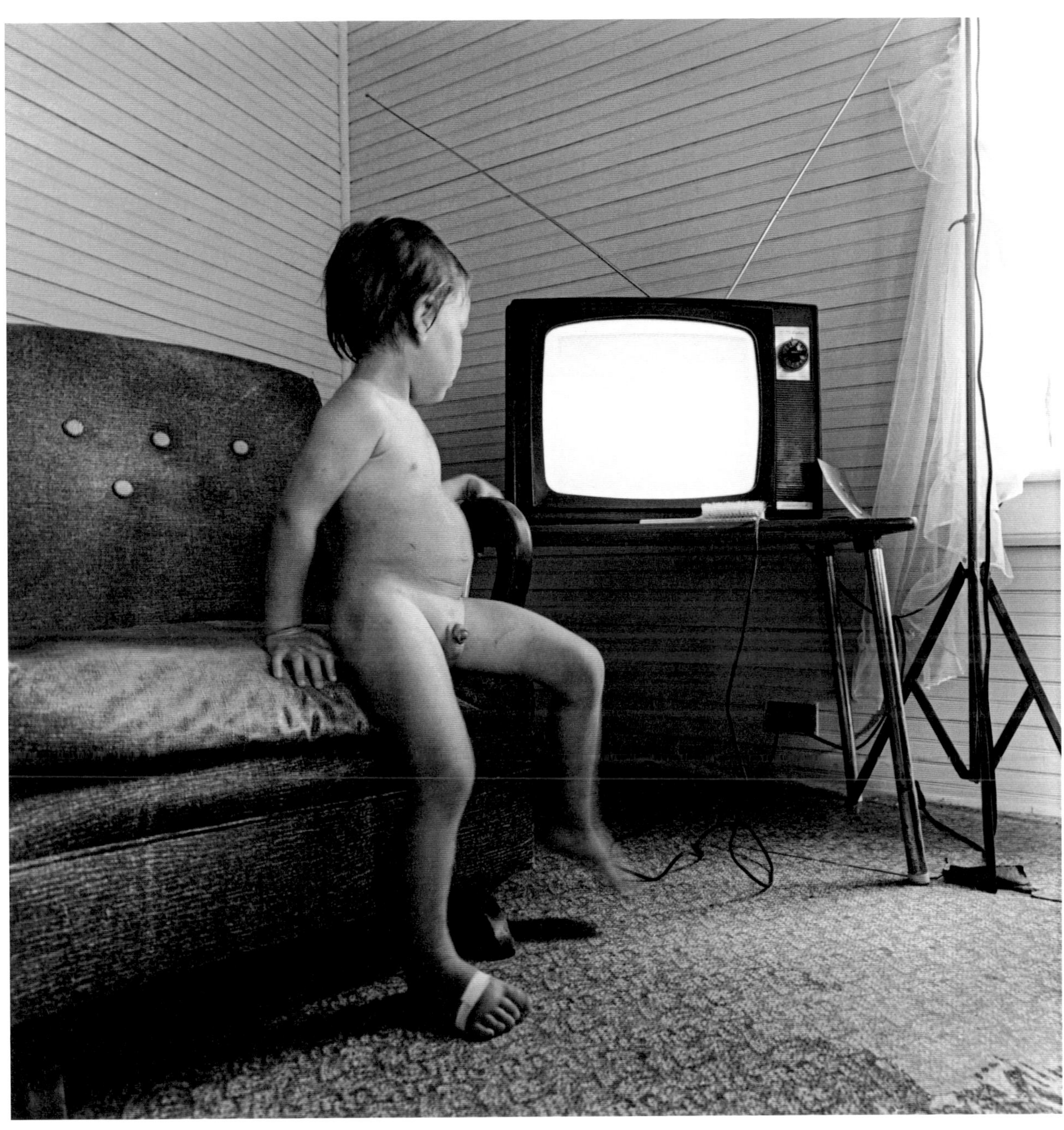

Elijah, Danville, 1970

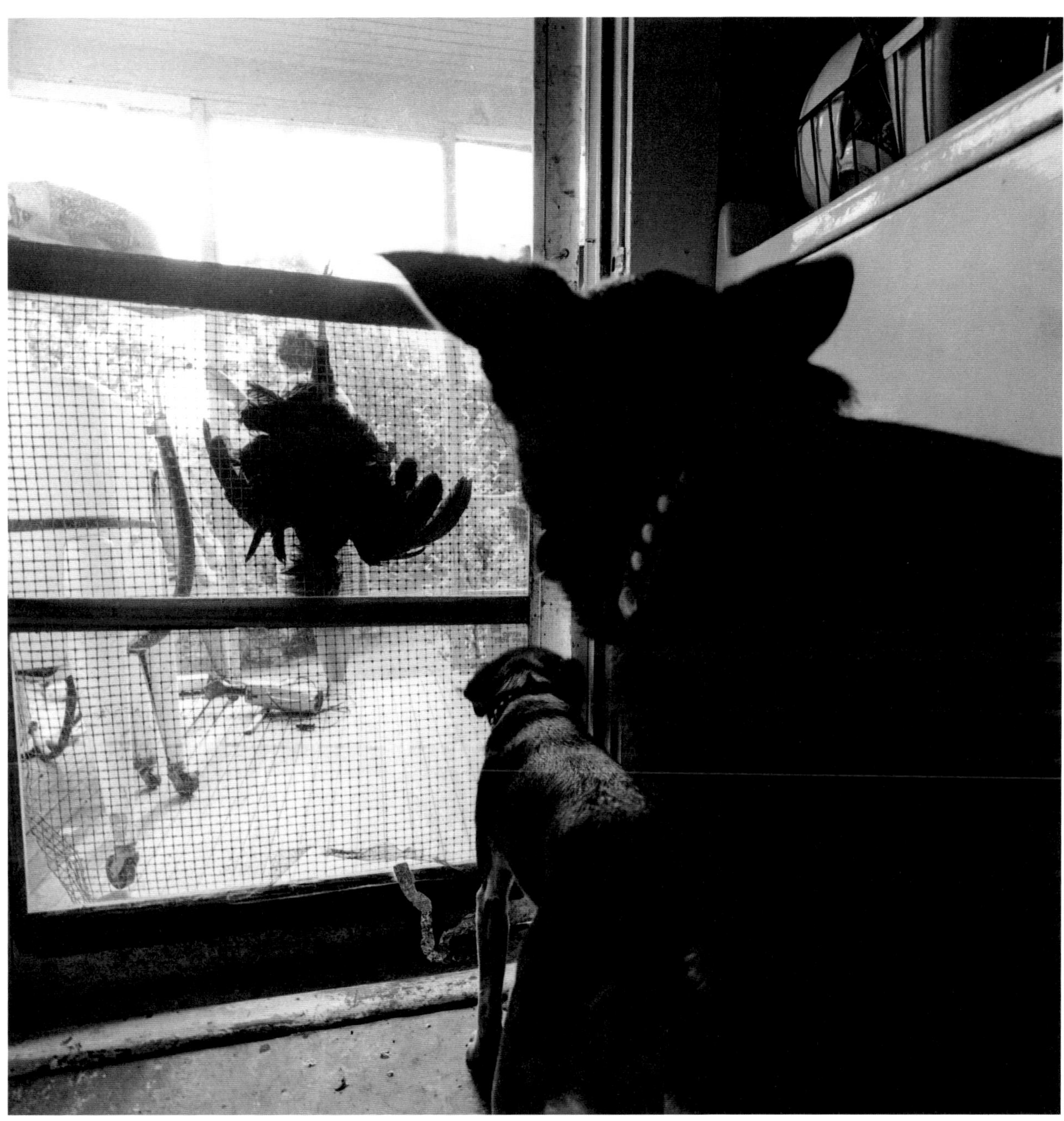

Reva's Dogs Looking, Danville, 1970

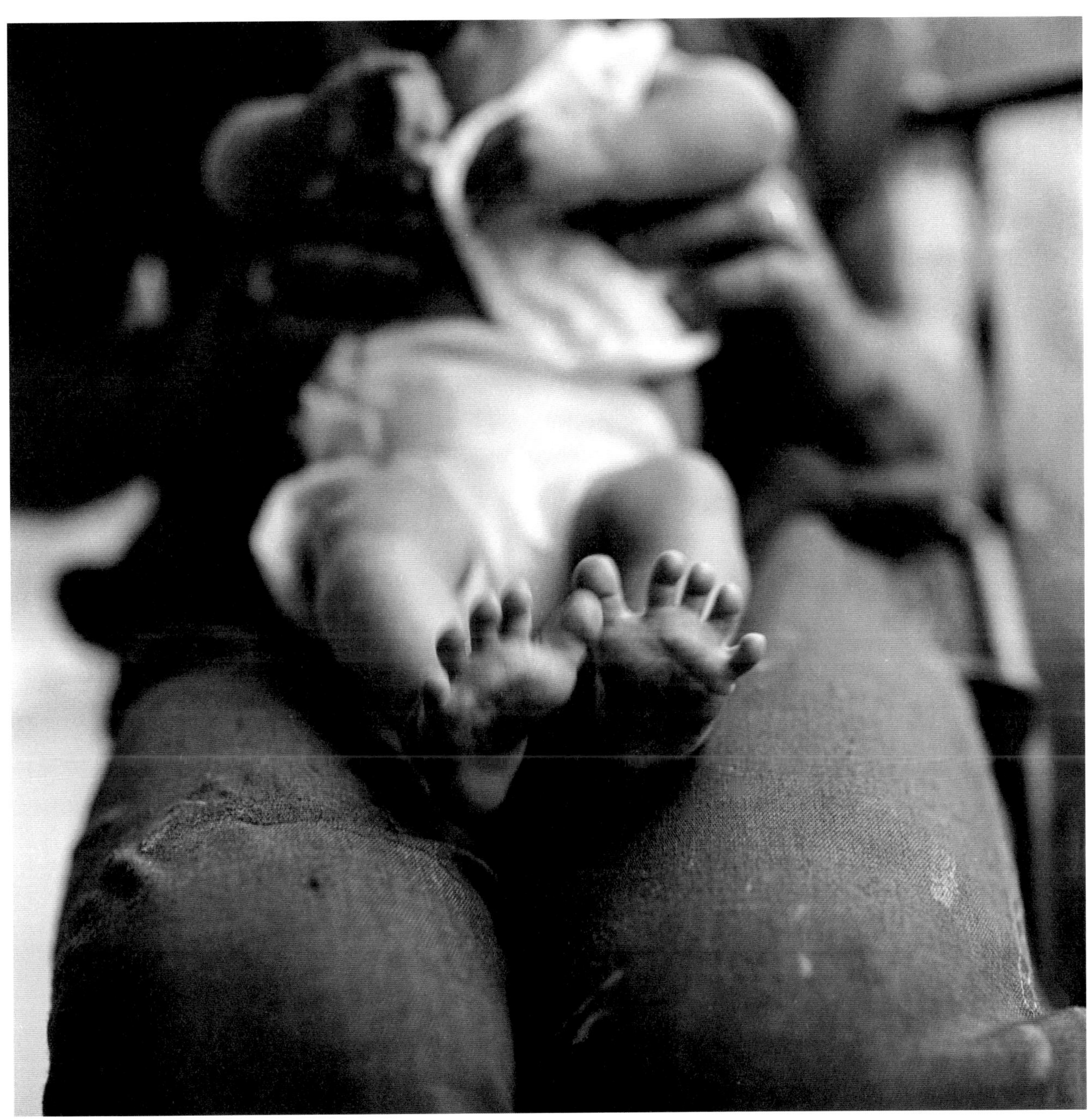

David, Holding Vincent, Danville, 1980

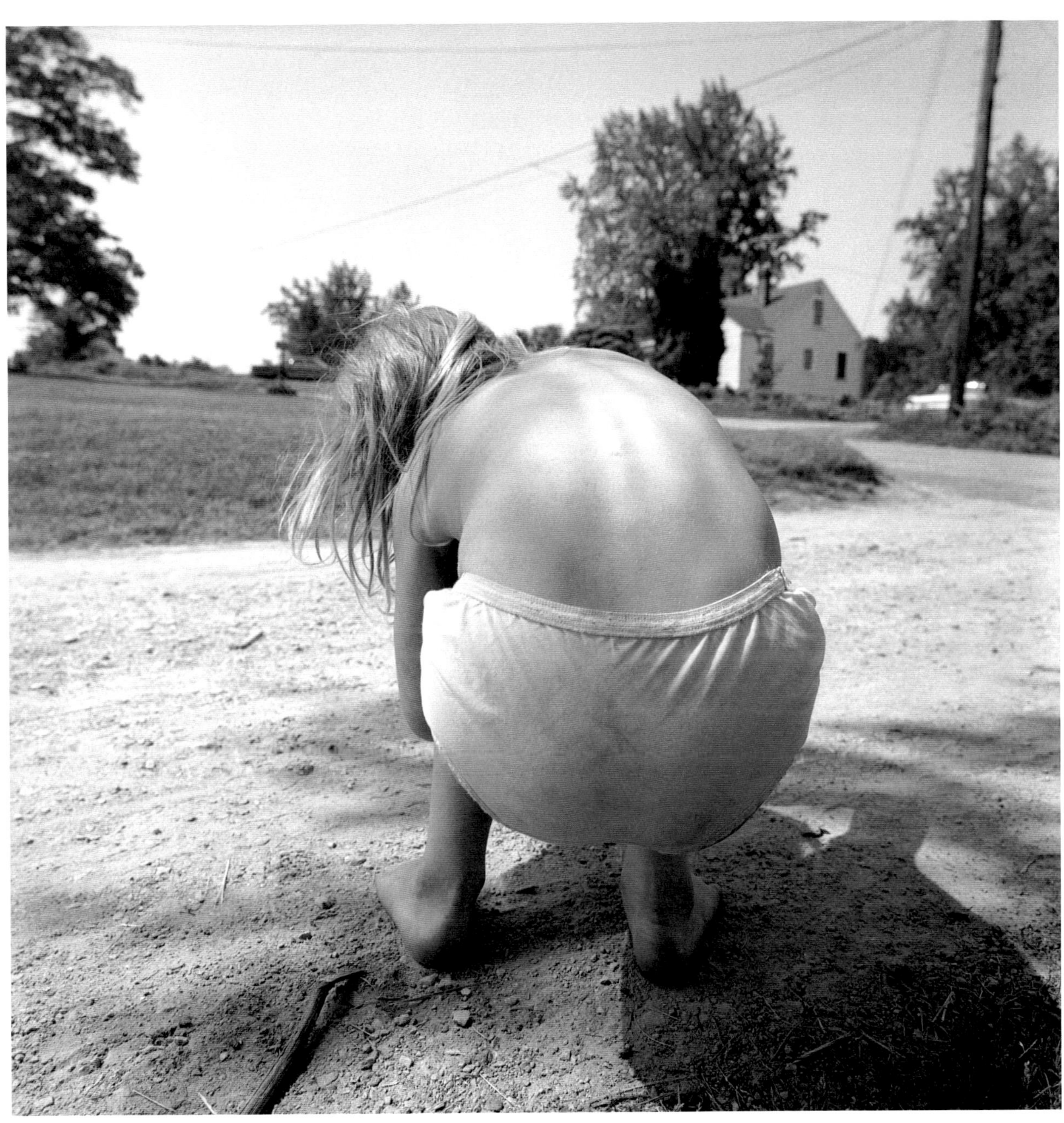

Donna Jo, Danville, 1970

I would not have understood how good this picture was when I was young, but now I think of it as being exquisitely beautiful. The shadow, and the space between her arm and her body, and the shadow's thinness, and the shape of the arm shadow and the strands of hair, and what's probably an apple twig in her hair. Elijah's behind her, poking out. And it is just the incarnation of Eve with apples. Eve authoring apples. You don't have to know it's apples, but I do.

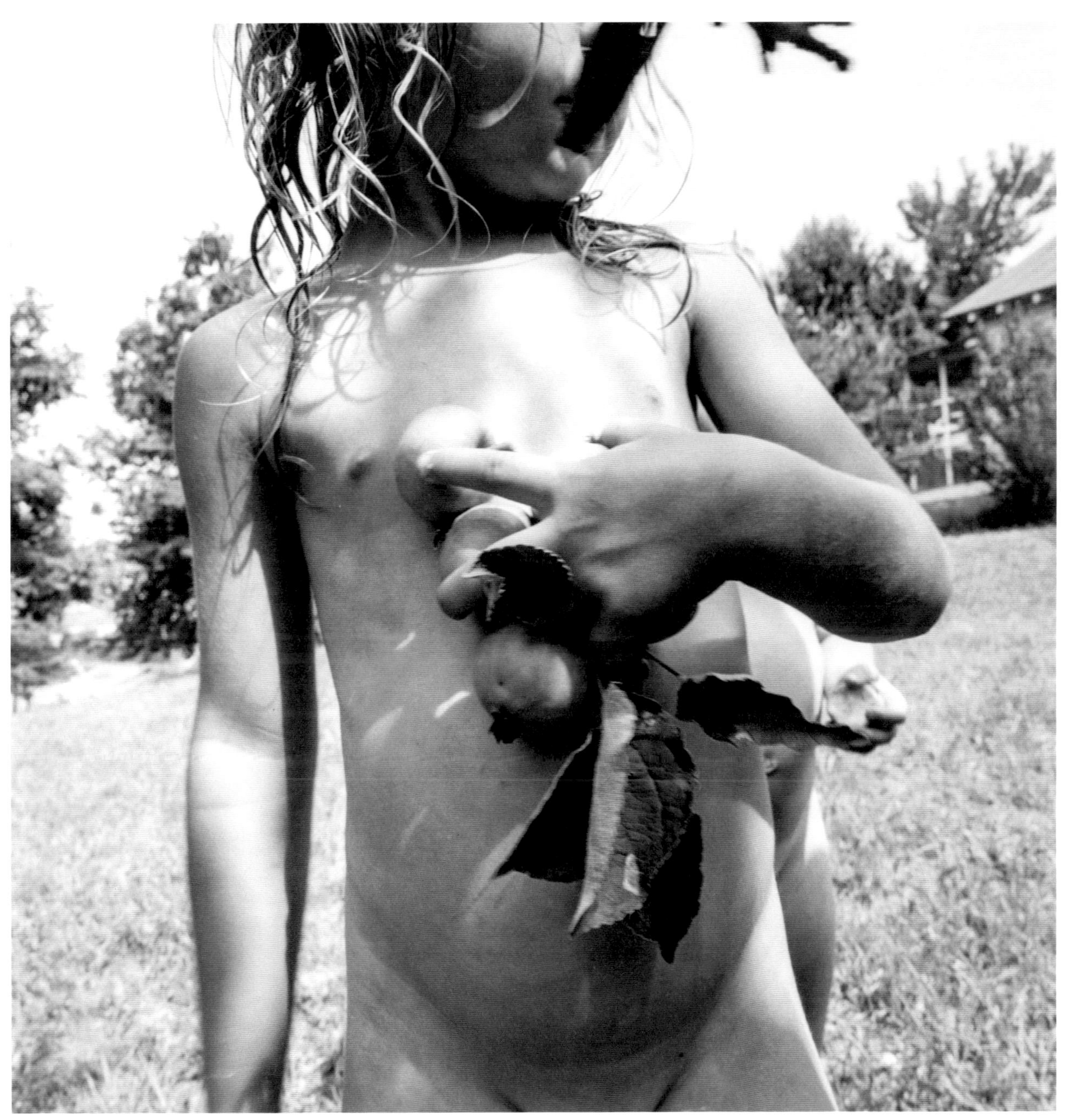

Donna Jo, Danville, 1970

Once you get into your adult experience, you can't help but see what you know. And you tend to bring adult vision to everything. But I think when this picture was made, I would only have seen what was happening there. I was just photographing the real moment. No symbolism. Look at the beautiful way the water is a steady stream until it reaches about eighty-nine degrees. Then it breaks up and you can watch the spaces between drops. Beautiful math.

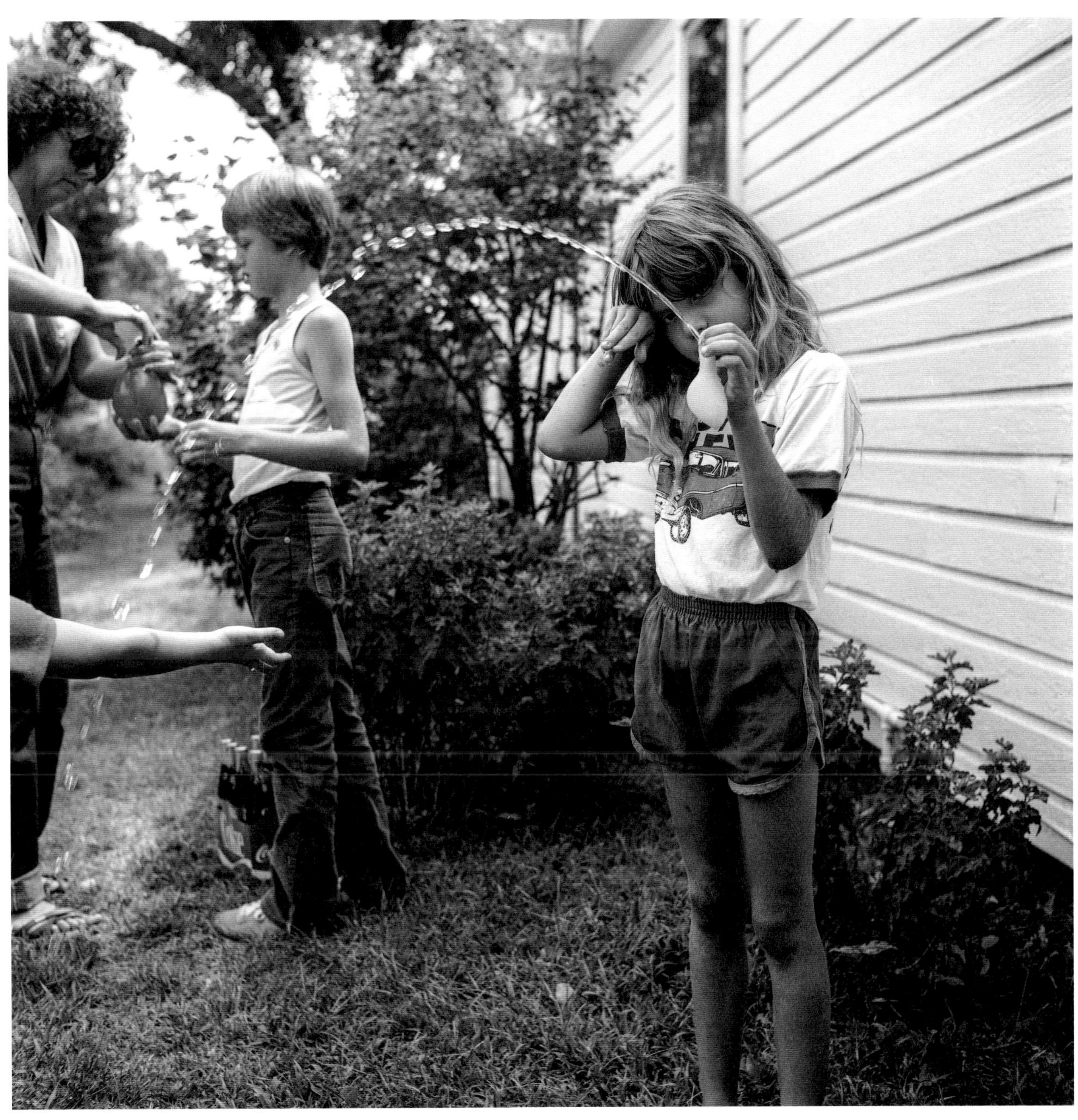

Family Reunion, Danville, 1983

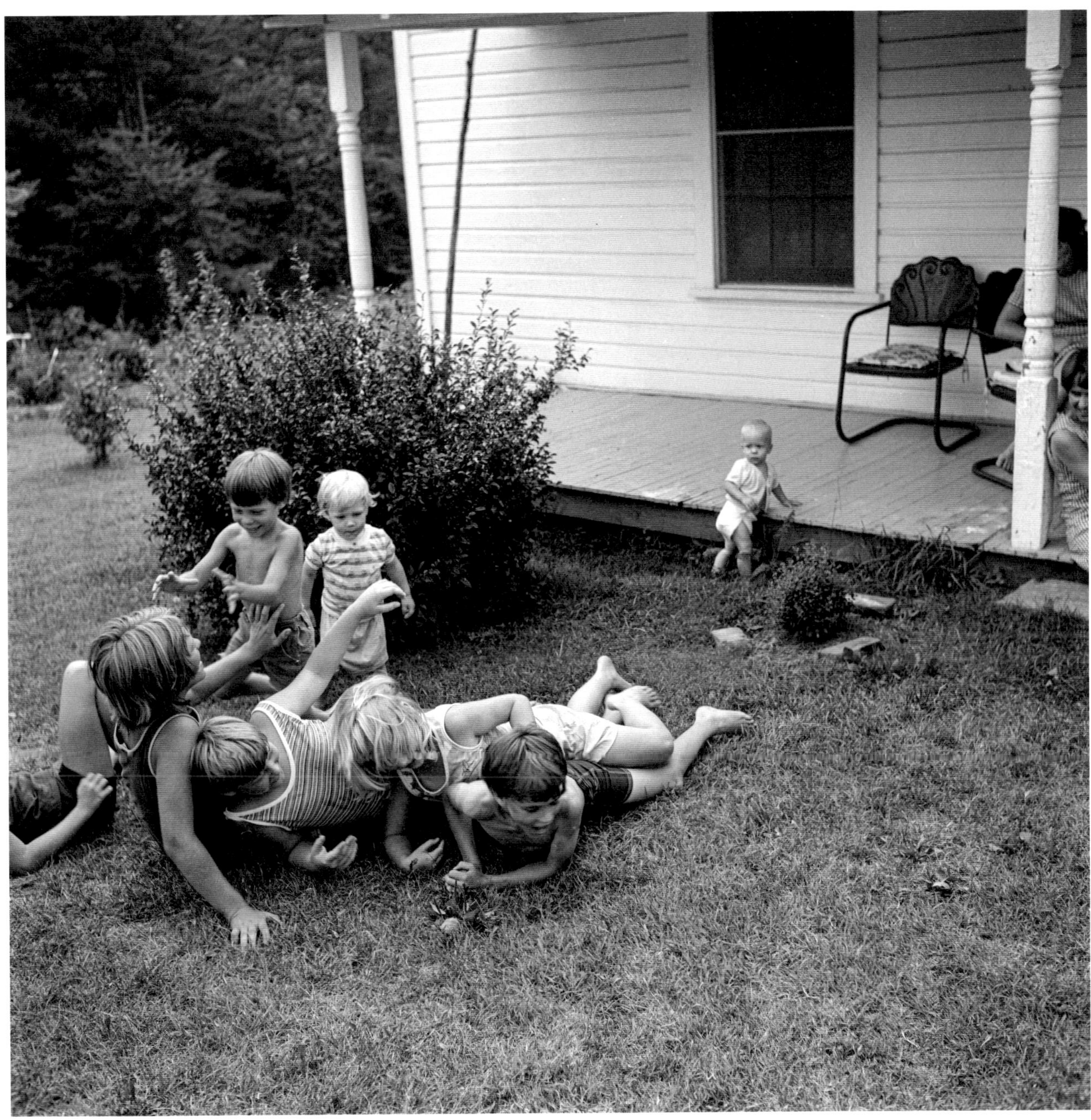

Children's Games, Danville, 1976

Nancy was born summer of 1960—the same day as our Isaac was born, but that was fourteen years later. I think she's fifteen here. It's one of the few pictures here that's just somebody addressing the camera. Years ago we would get requests to use an image of Nancy on a record cover. We all agreed to not having family pictures on anything commercial. However, some years later, Nancy, almost out of nowhere, said, "But if Jon Bon Jovi asks to use my picture, you let him use it, OK?"

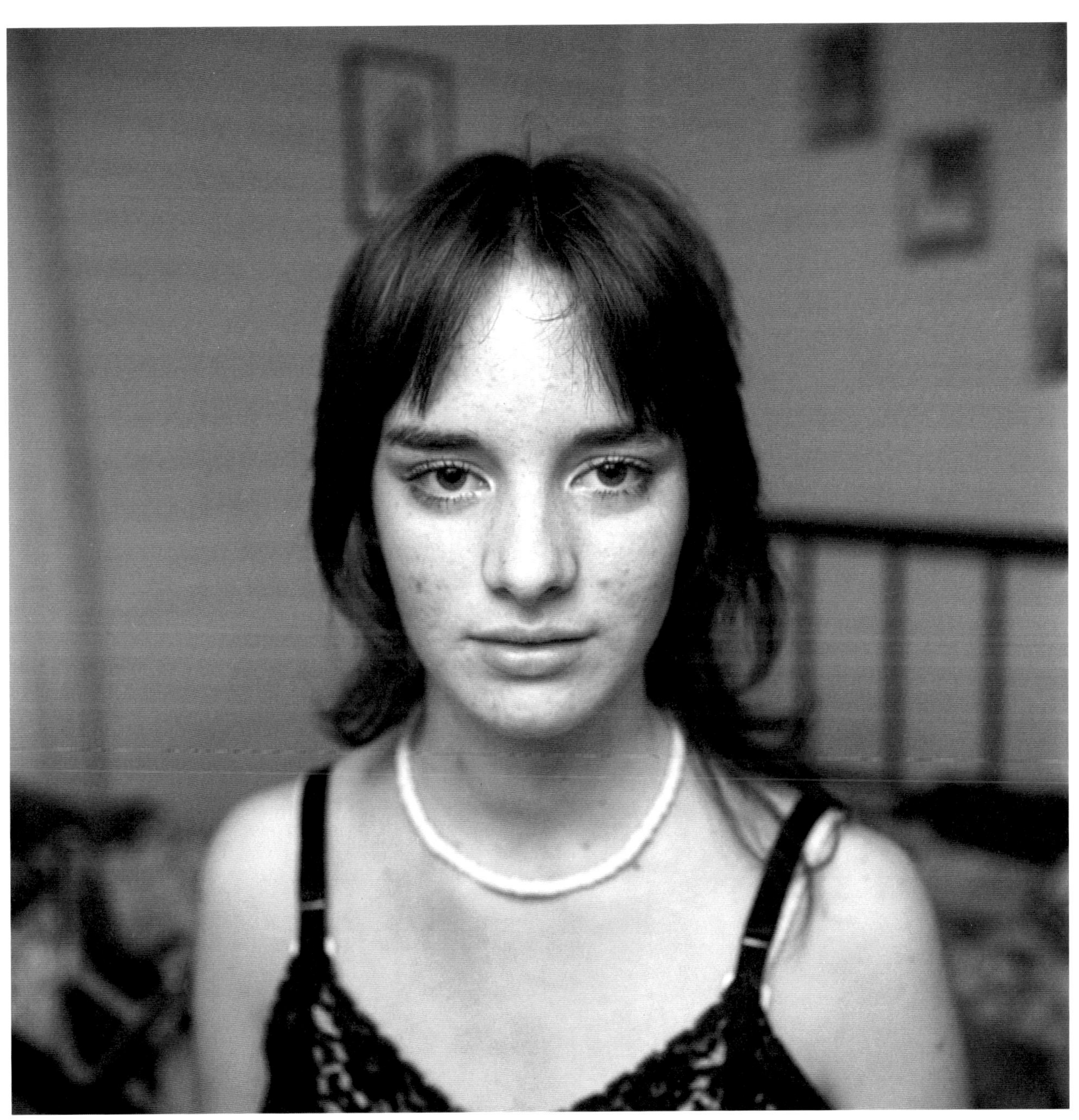

Nancy at Fifteen, Danville, 1975

When the children were playing in the yard, I sometimes had to go inside to load my Rolleiflex, afraid that it was too bright outside. I would take the old film out, load it, and run back outside as quickly as humanly possible, concerned that I'd miss something important. On days when things were happening, I might be taking seven, eight rolls of film in one huge deluge of wanting to see.

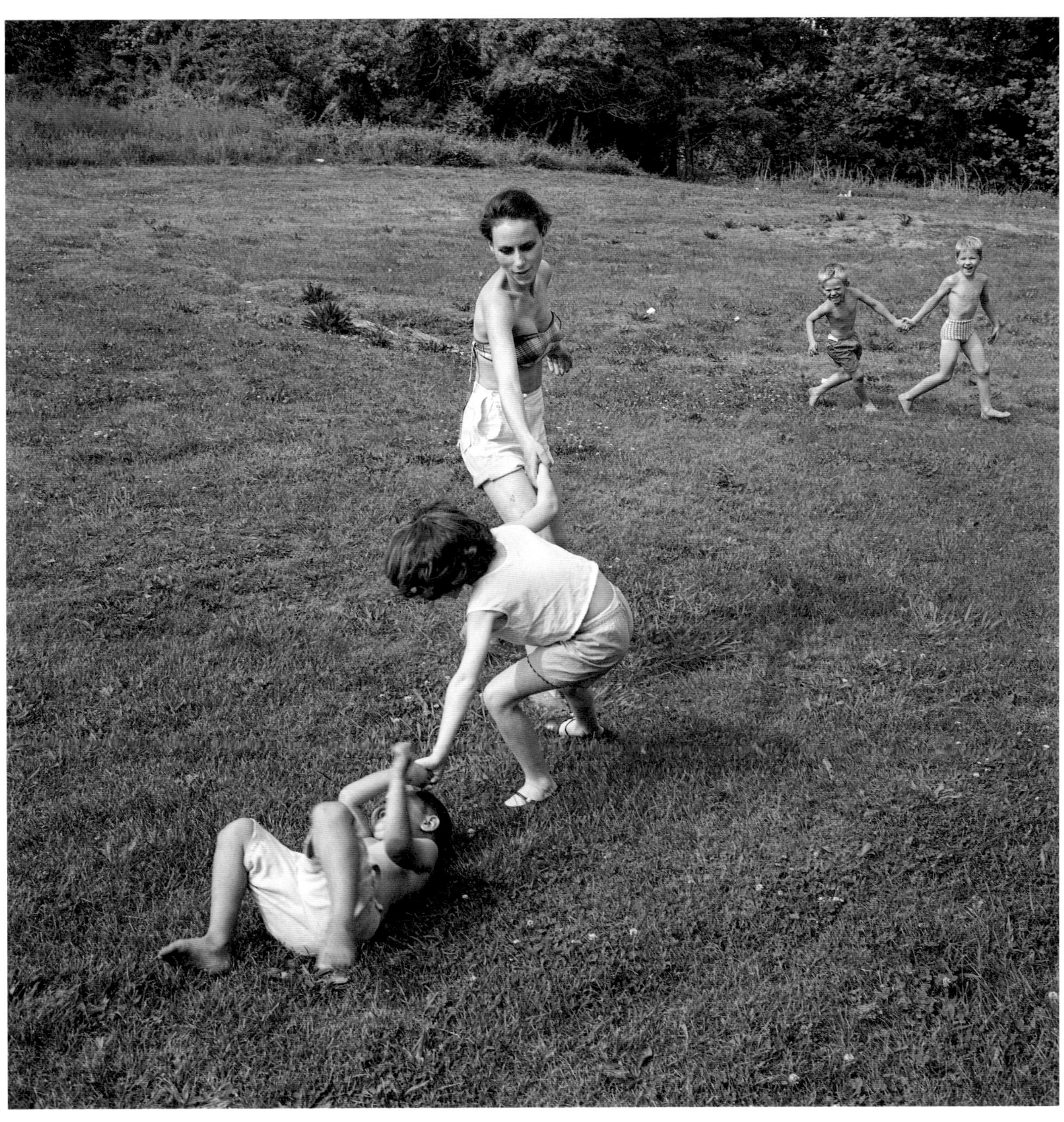

"Crack the Whip," Danville, 1966

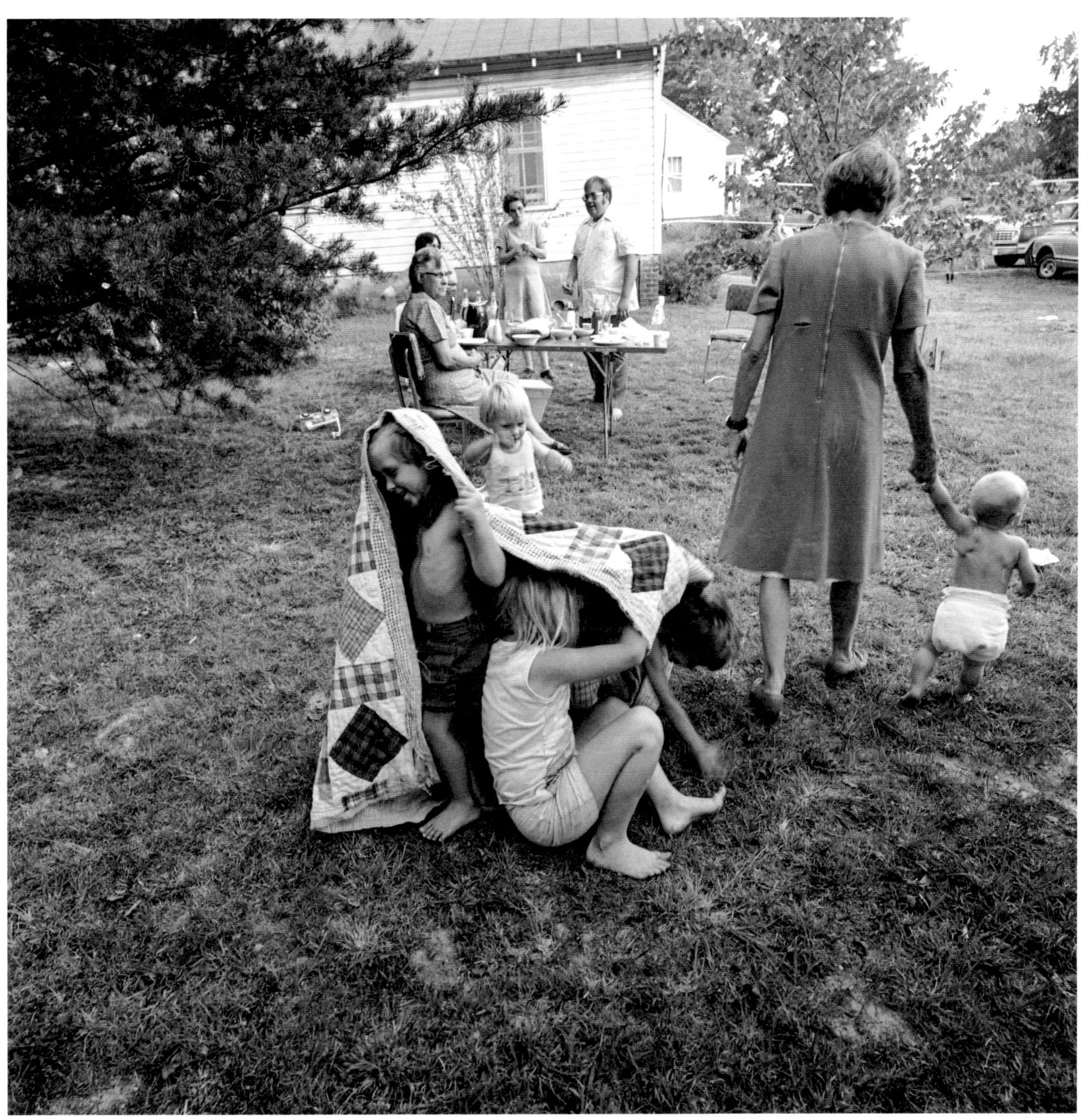

Family Picnic, Danville, 1976

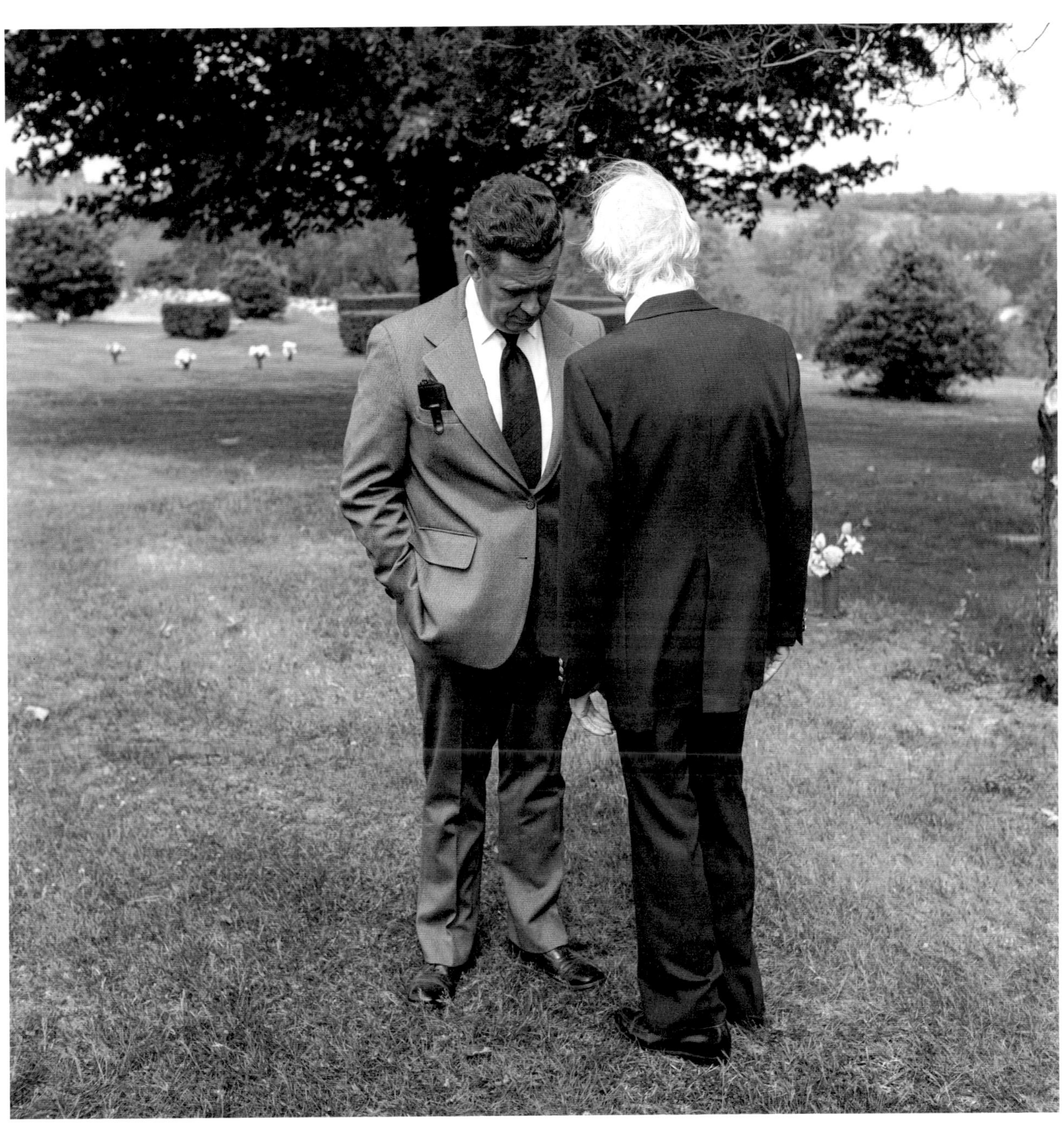

Lynchburg, Virginia, 1976

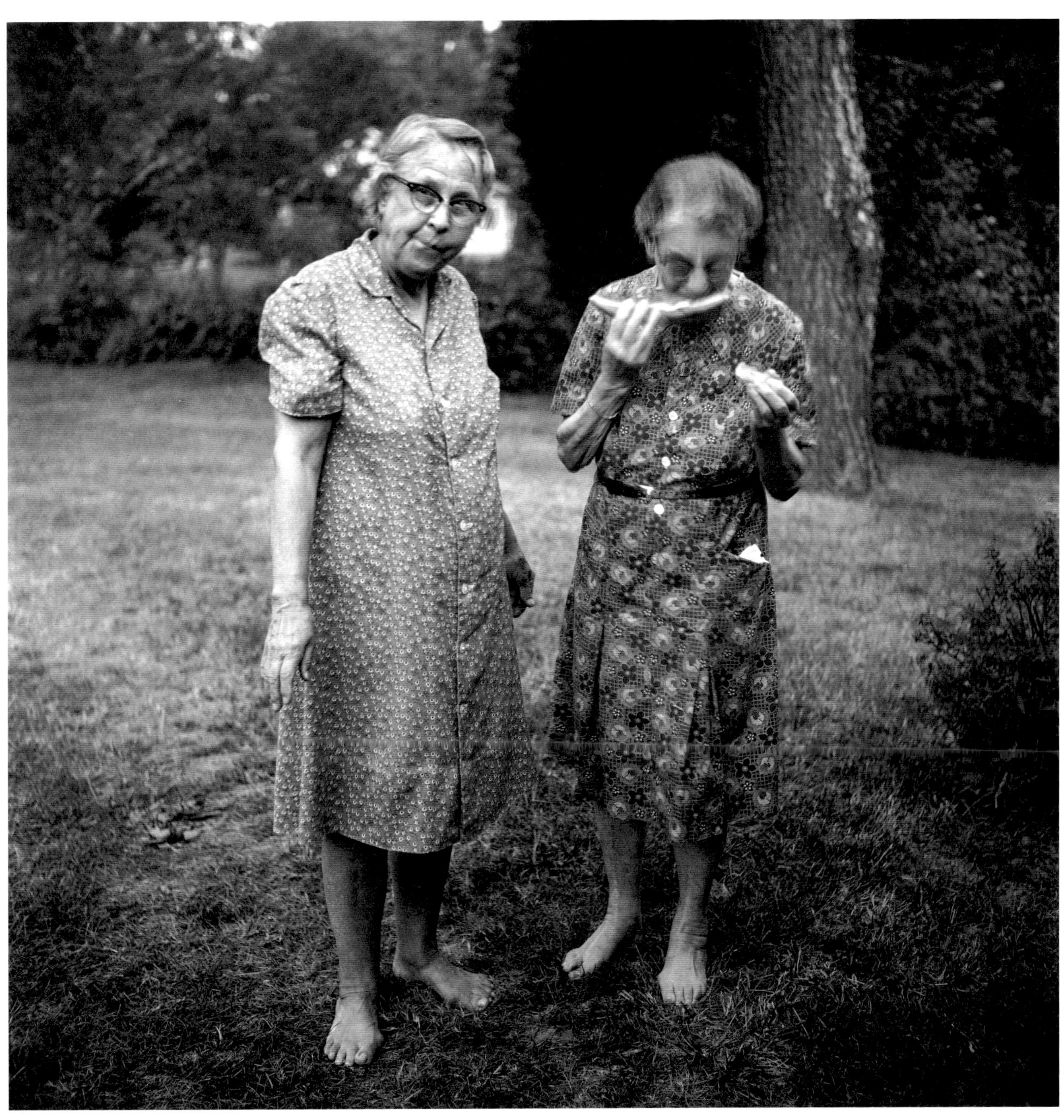

Aunt Gertrude and Fannie, Danville, 1982

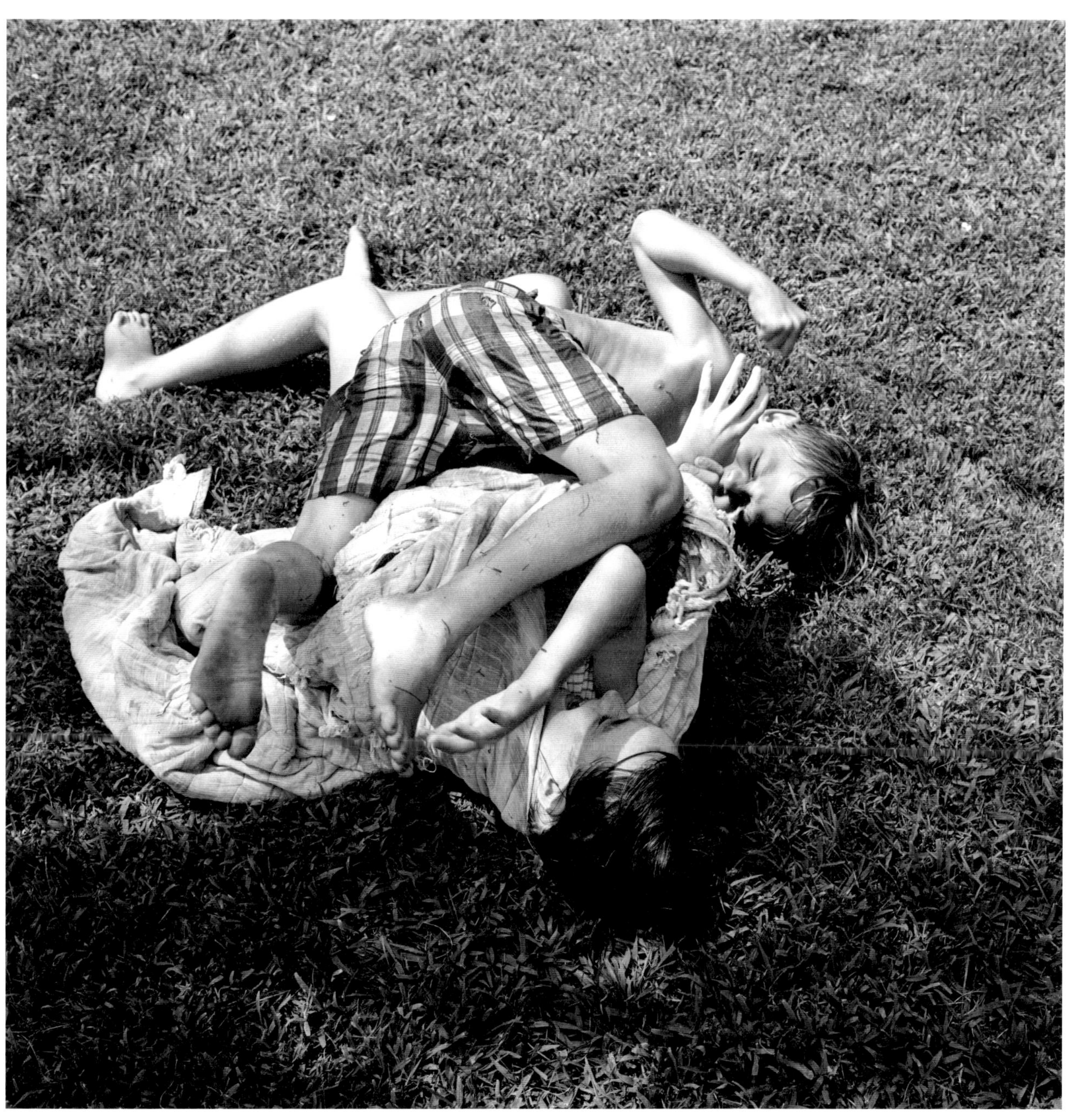

Nancy and Dwayne, Danville, 1971

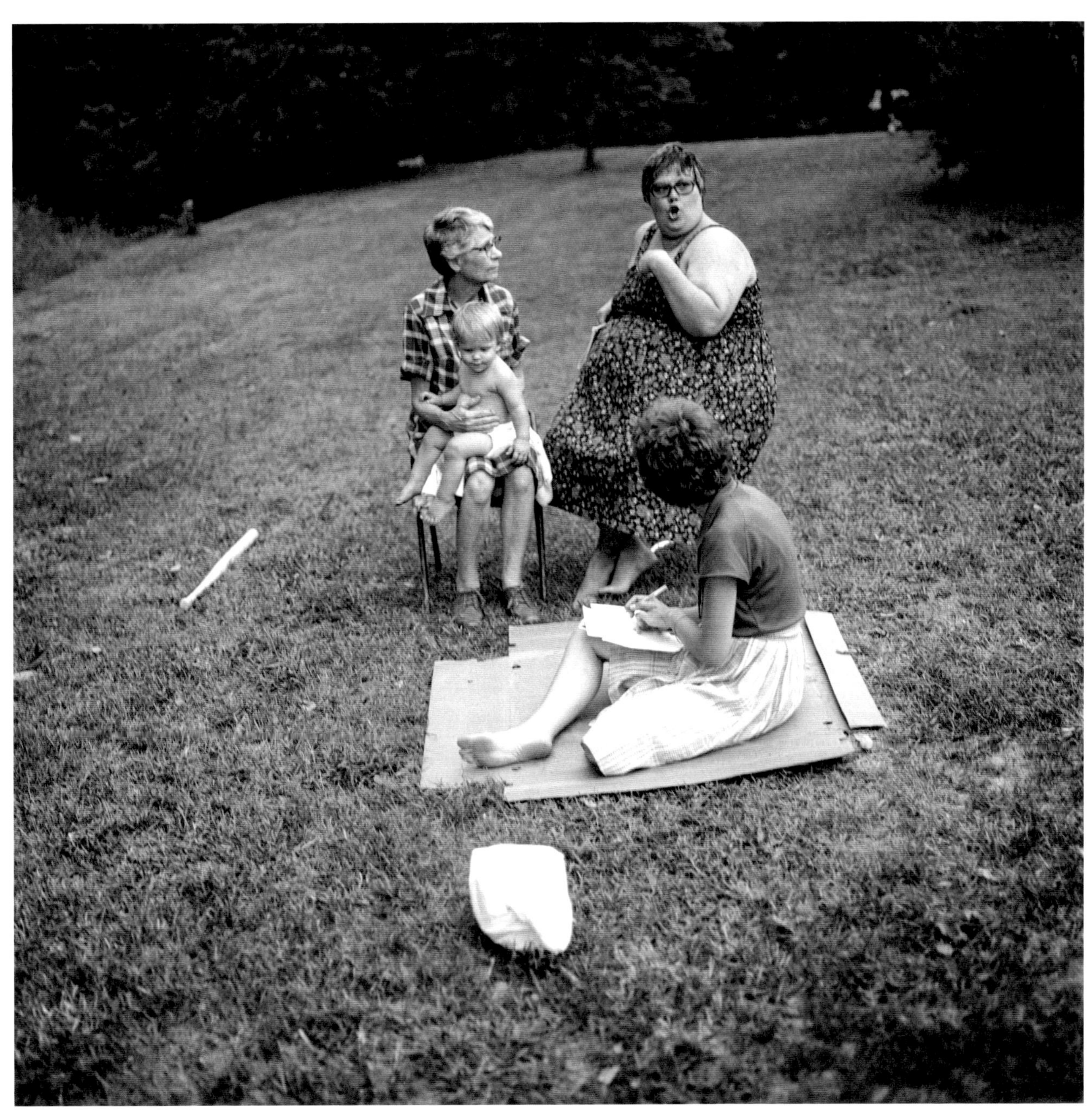

Reva Holding Baby Vincent, Dean and Mae, Danville, 1981

Ralph was a connoisseur of lawn mowing. He was a person of detail, and I think the picture of him has a touch of his sort of fastidiousness. He mowed everybody's yard. He rolled his own cigarettes, and he repaired radios and televisions, in which he was mostly self-schooled, although he also took a correspondence course in radio and TV.

In 1973, the day Ralph's father was buried, we had just driven in from Pennsylvania. And when I walked in the front door, he said, "Sit down. I have something to tell you." And I sat down and he said, "After people are married and live together a long time, sleeping in the same bed every night, your head is right there next to that other person. You know, there are waves, and information is exchanged between those heads, even when you're sleeping; they know things and they may not know how they know, but that information is transferred between one human and another when they're that close." And then, as if there was a semicolon between that sentence and this one, he said, "You realize—probably you don't—that you can mow that graveyard with a 22-inch mower more efficiently than with a 24-inch mower?"

And I had to say, "Ralph, I had never thought of that. That is very specialized information, but I'm happy to learn both of those things." And you see, I've remembered them to this day. I've often thought that he was under the pressure of eternity, but also the weight of mortality was bearing down for a moment or two, and he was conscious of some eternal knowledge he had that somehow might be necessary or useful, if he's to pass from this life on to the next. I think there is a psychological need to use or share your secret wisdom before it's lost.

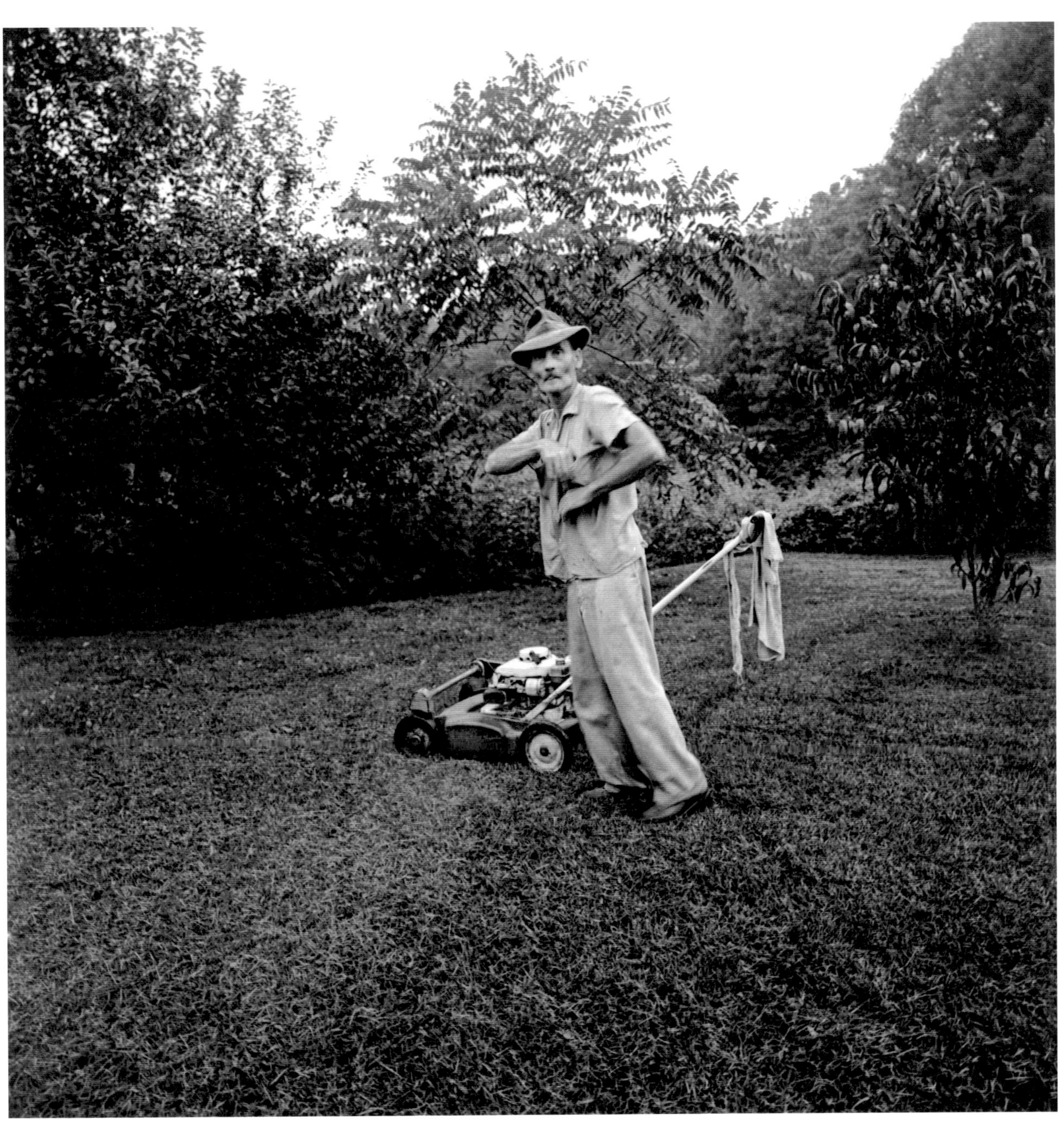

Ralph Booher, Danville, 1971

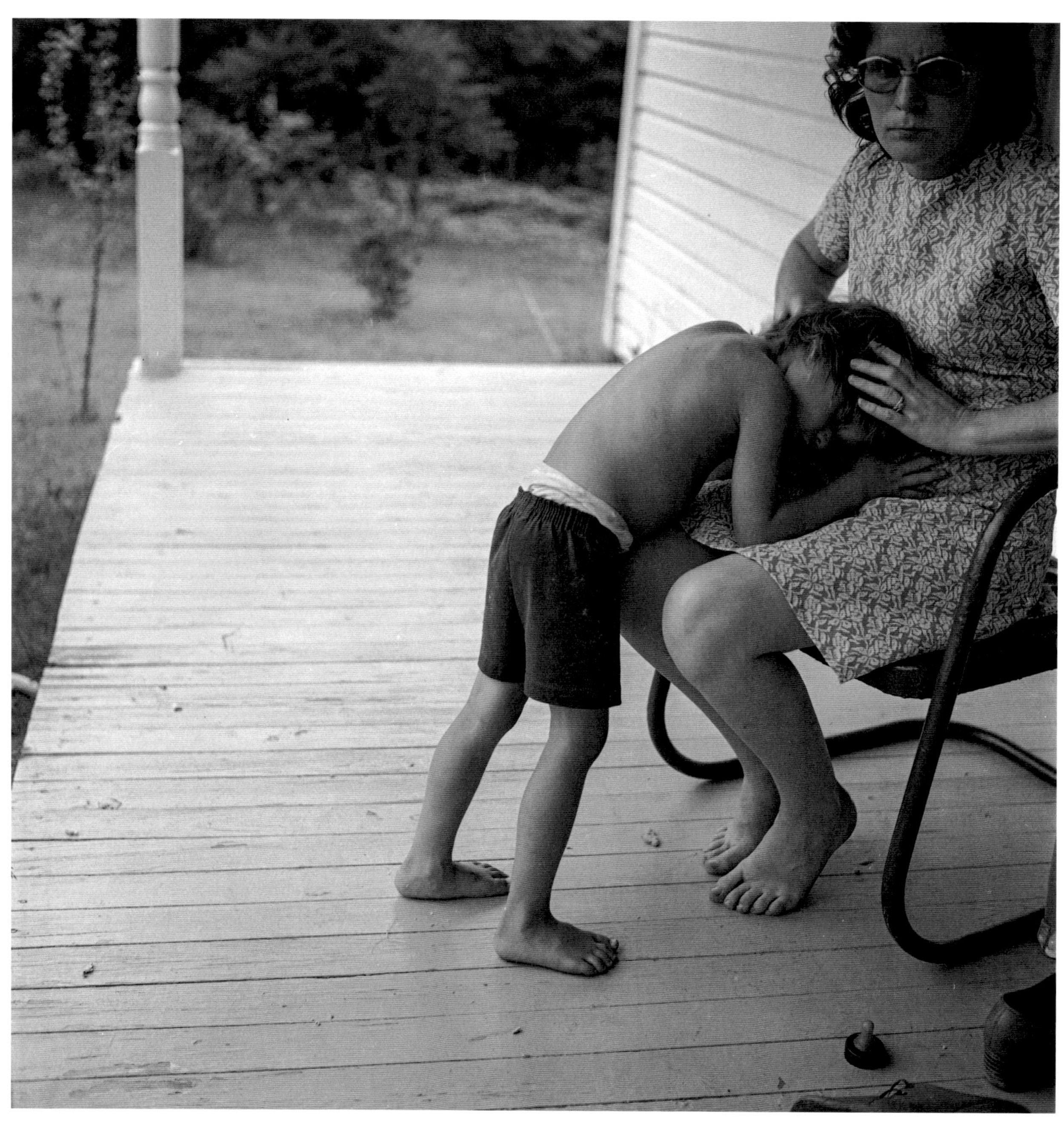

Helen and John David, Danville, 1976

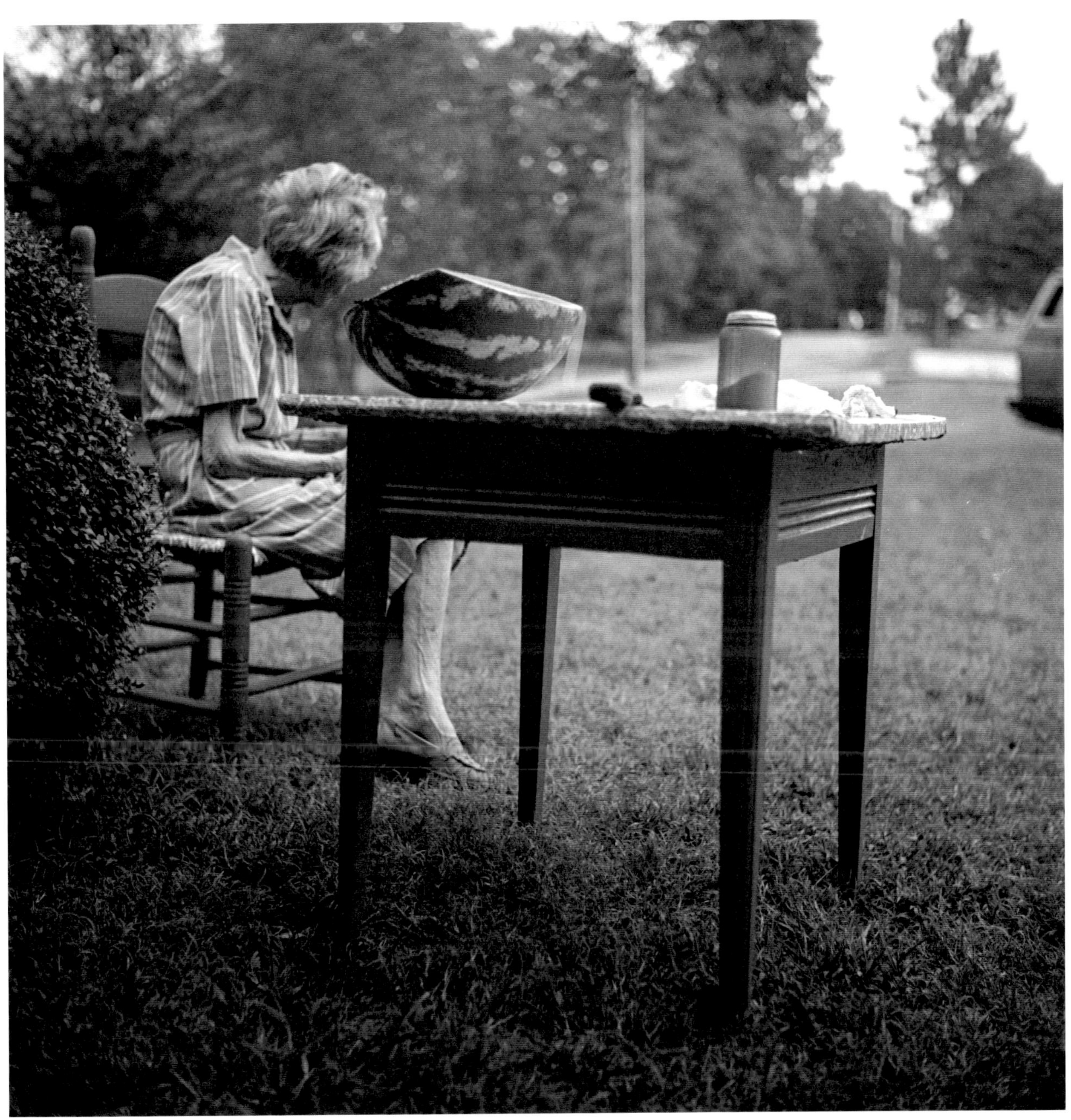

Reva, Danville, 1994

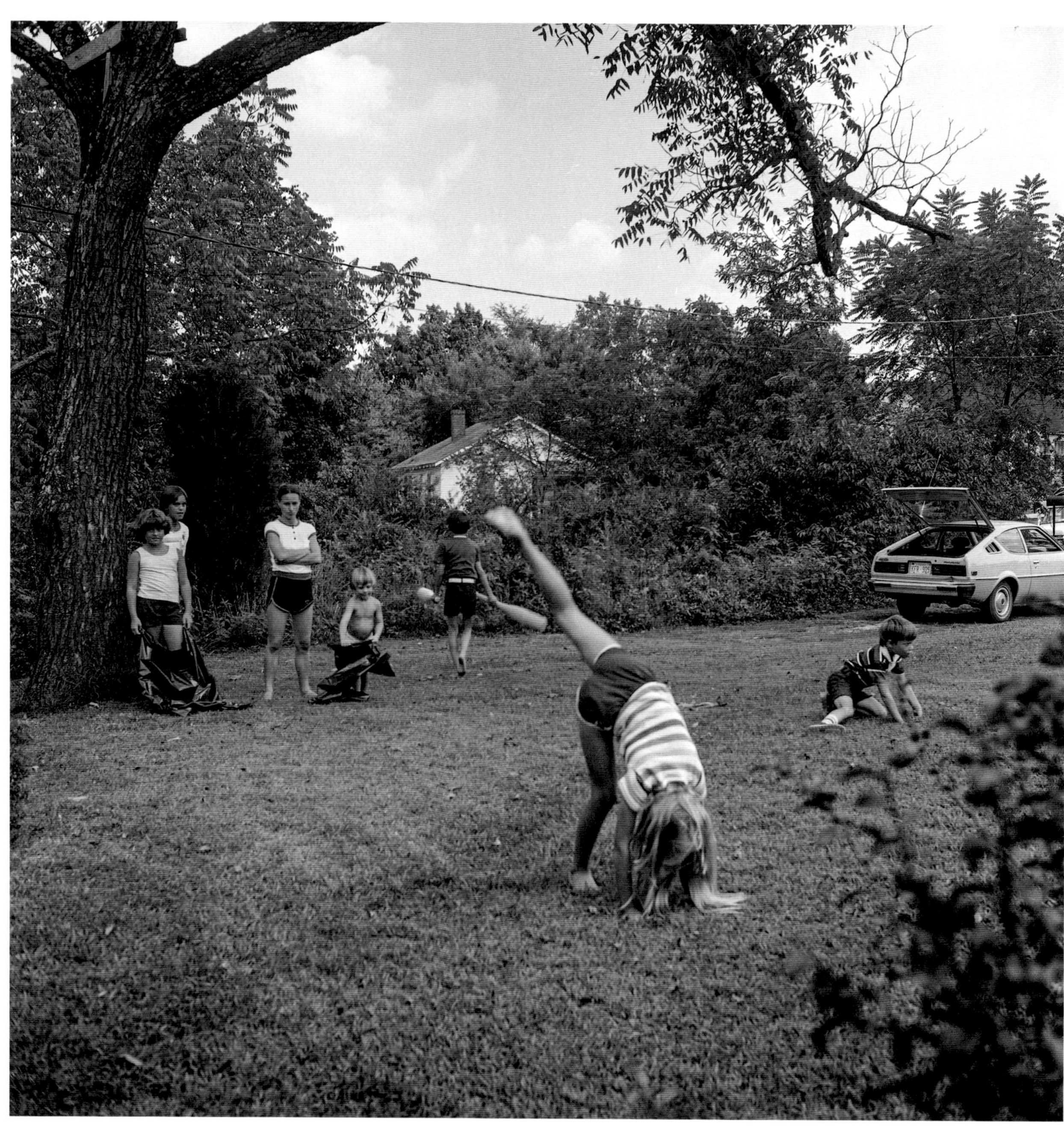

Children's Games, Danville, 1979

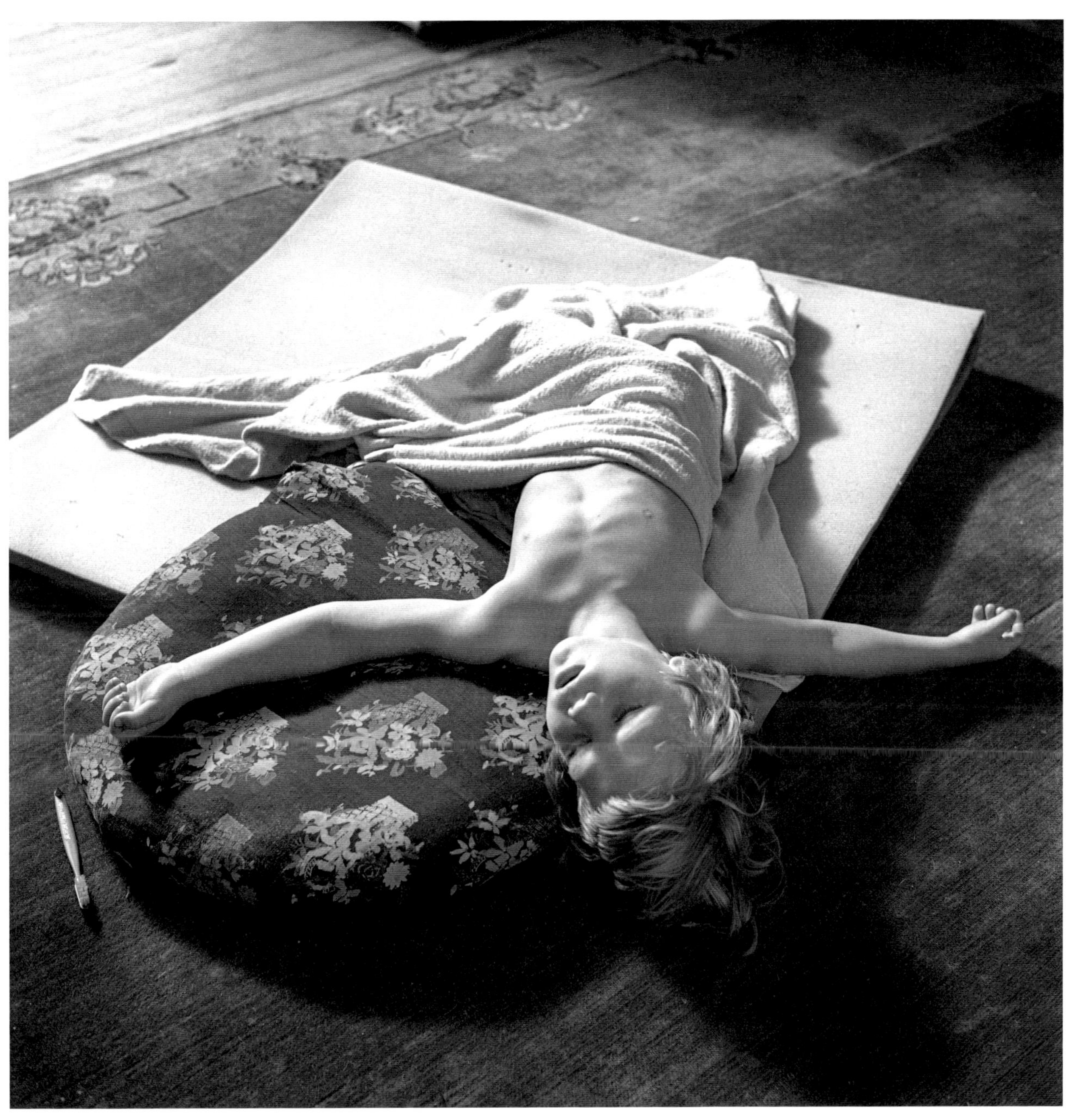

Isaac, Newtown, Pennsylvania, 1980

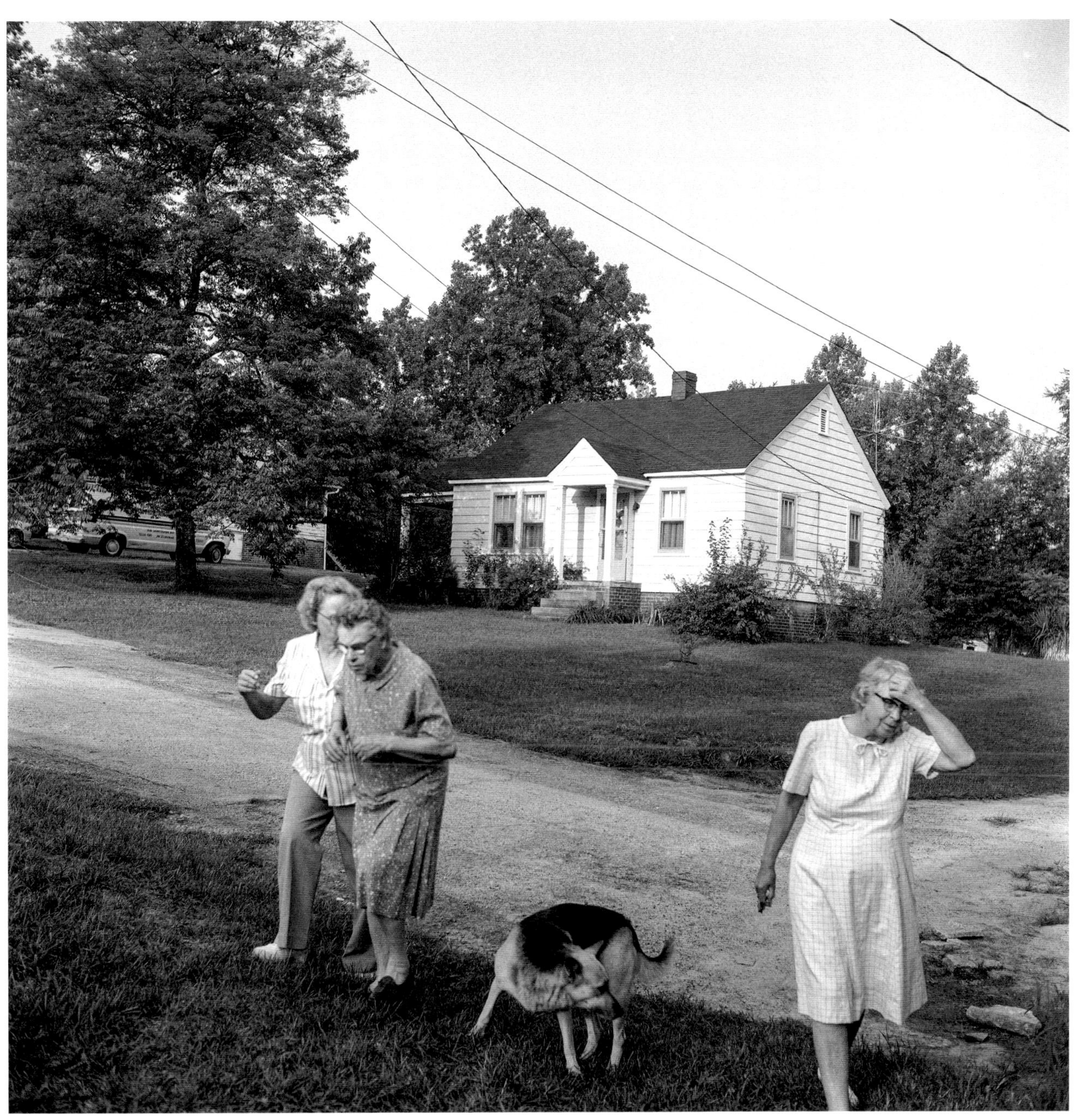

Bernice, Fannie, and Gertrude, 1986

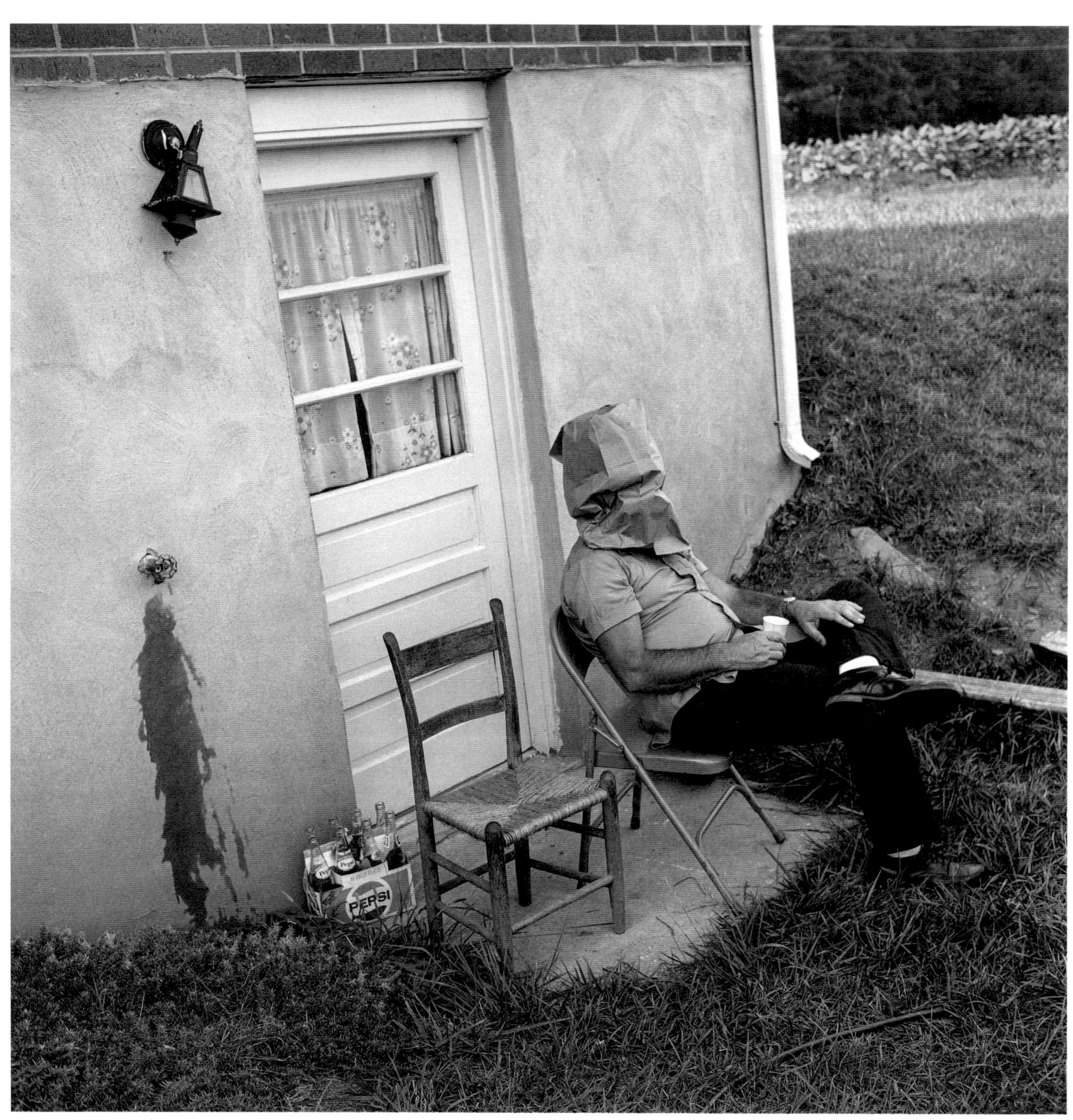

Luther, Chatham, Virginia, 1979

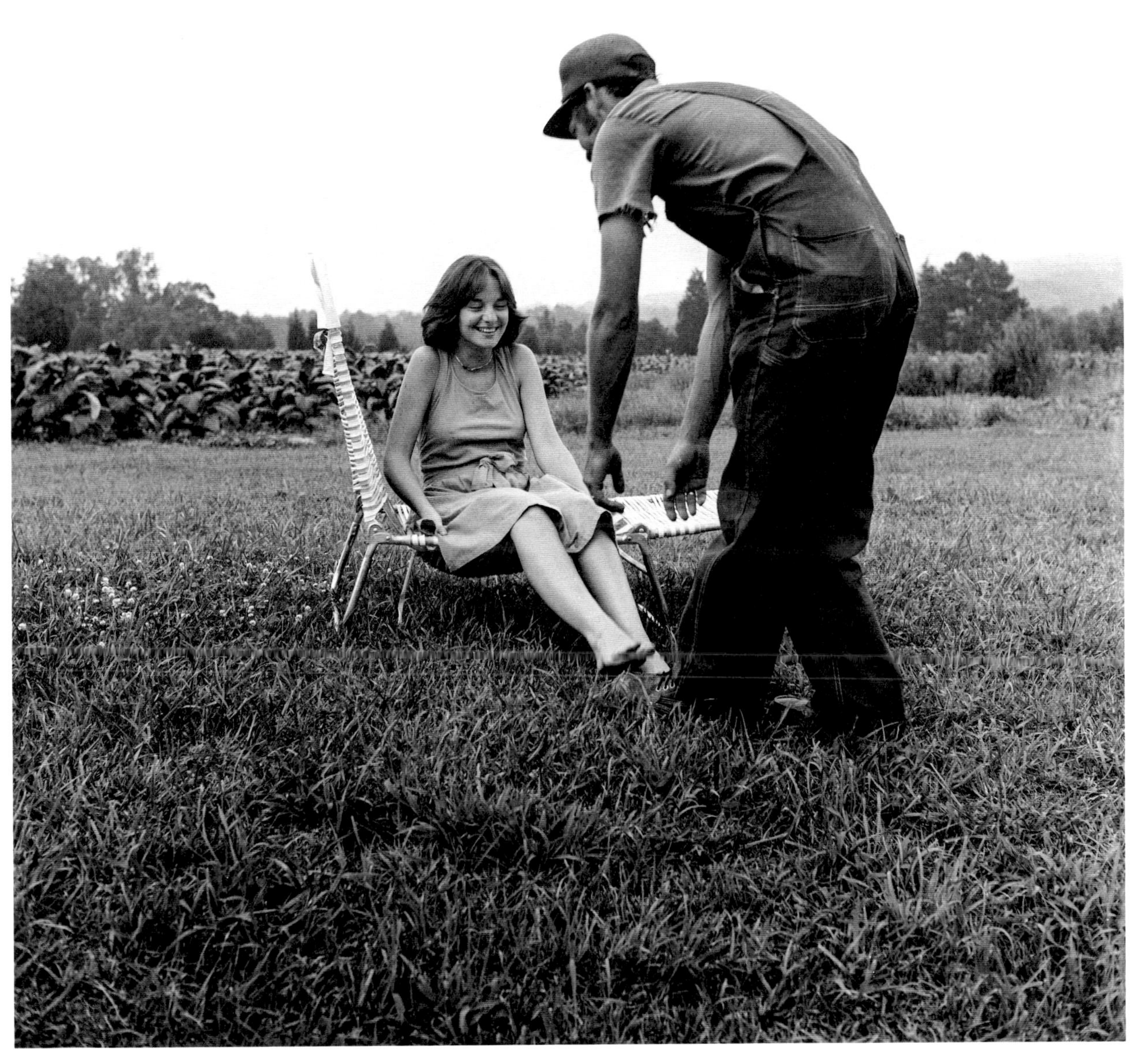

Nancy and David, Halifax, Virginia, 1979

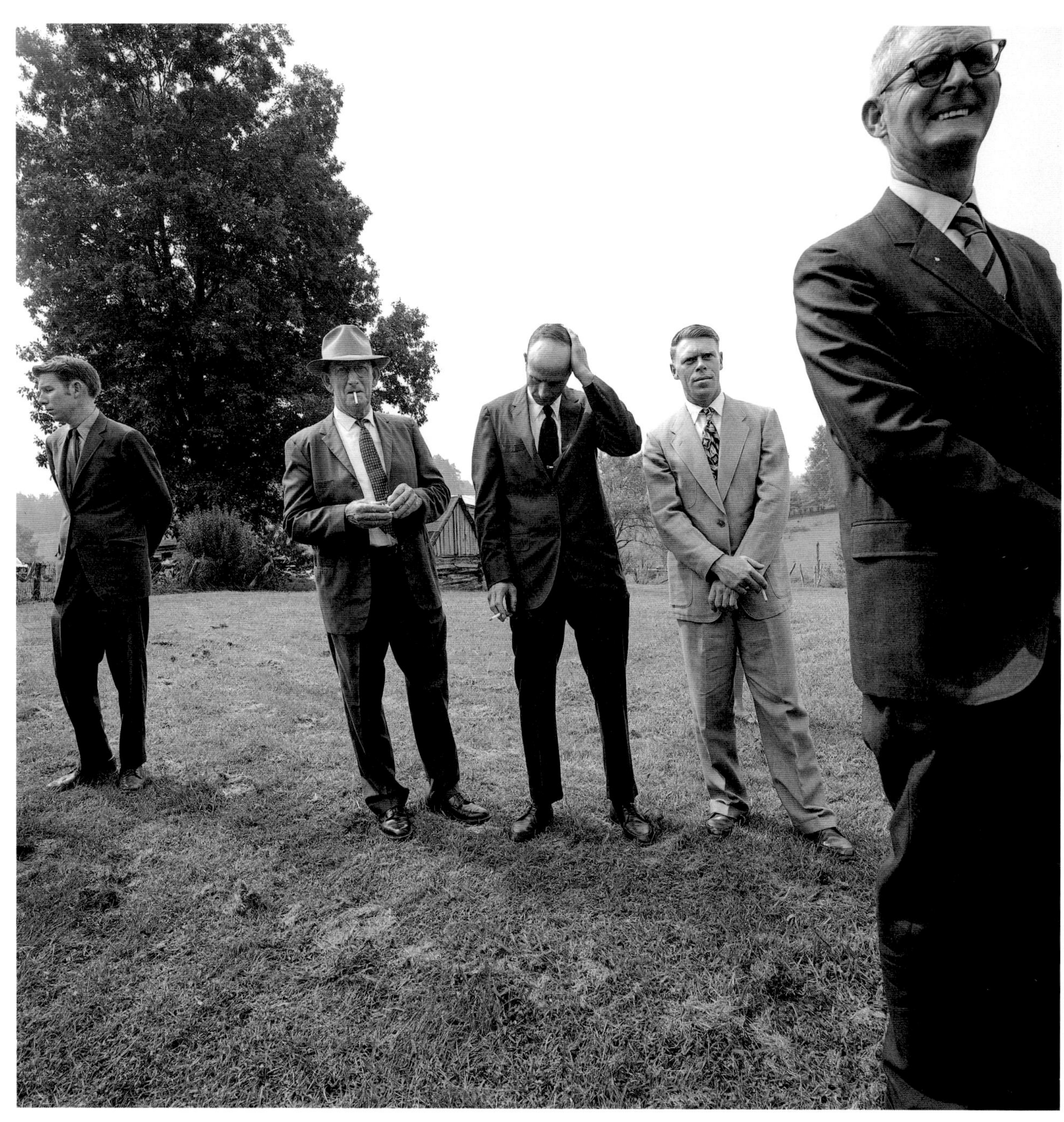

Funeral, Buckingham County, Virginia, 1971

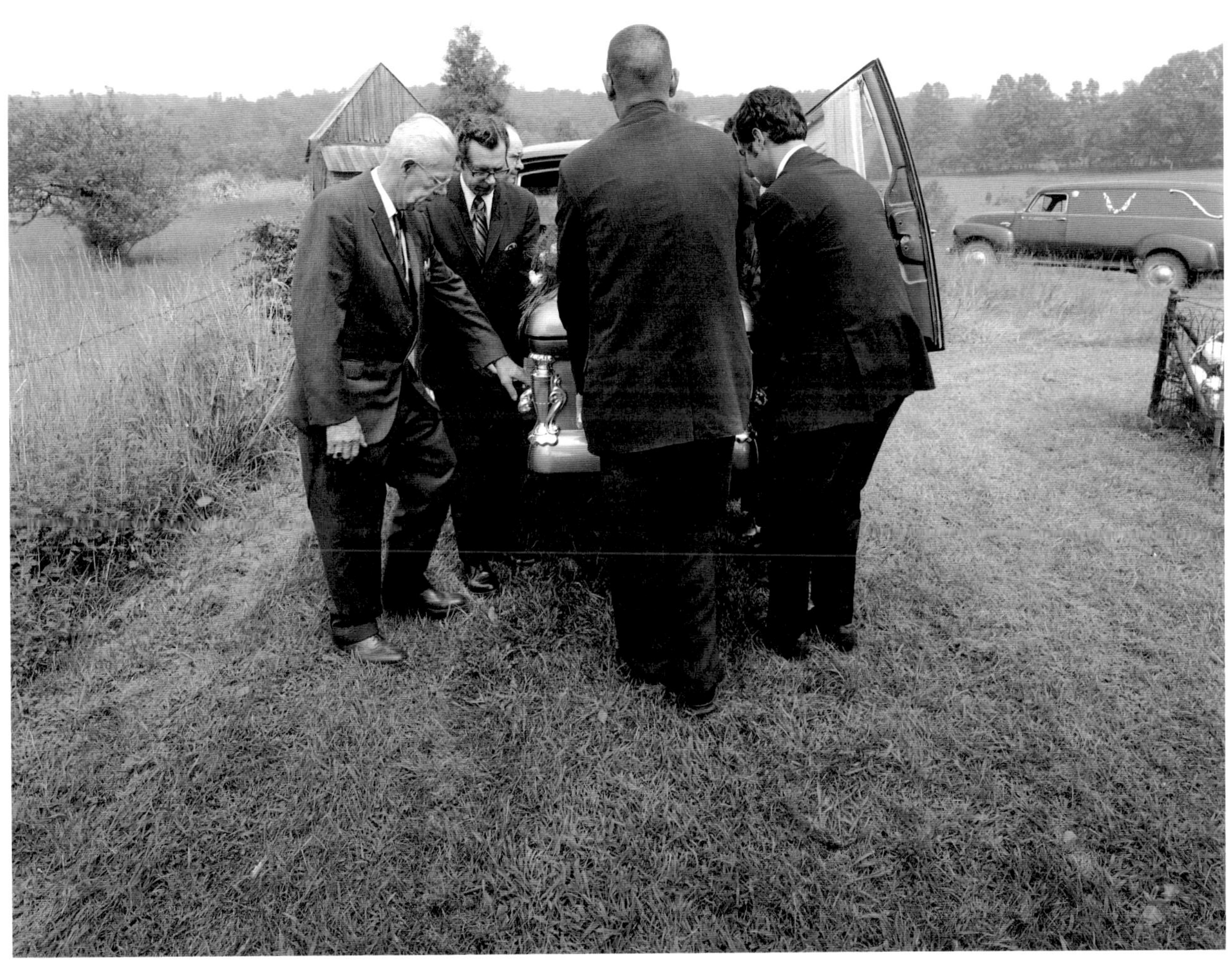

At the Gravesite, Buckingham County, Virginia, 1971

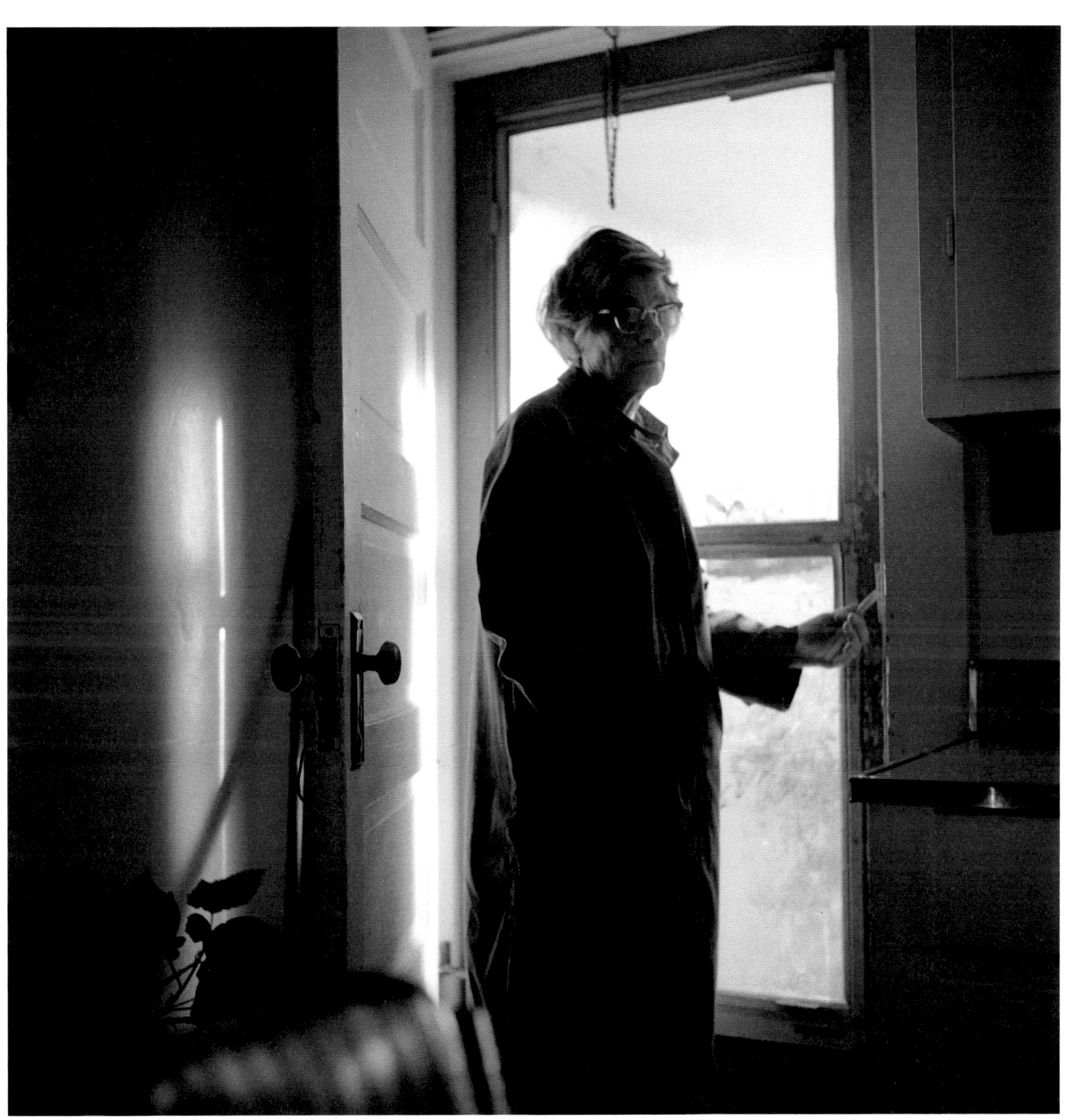

Reva Leaving, Danville, 1971

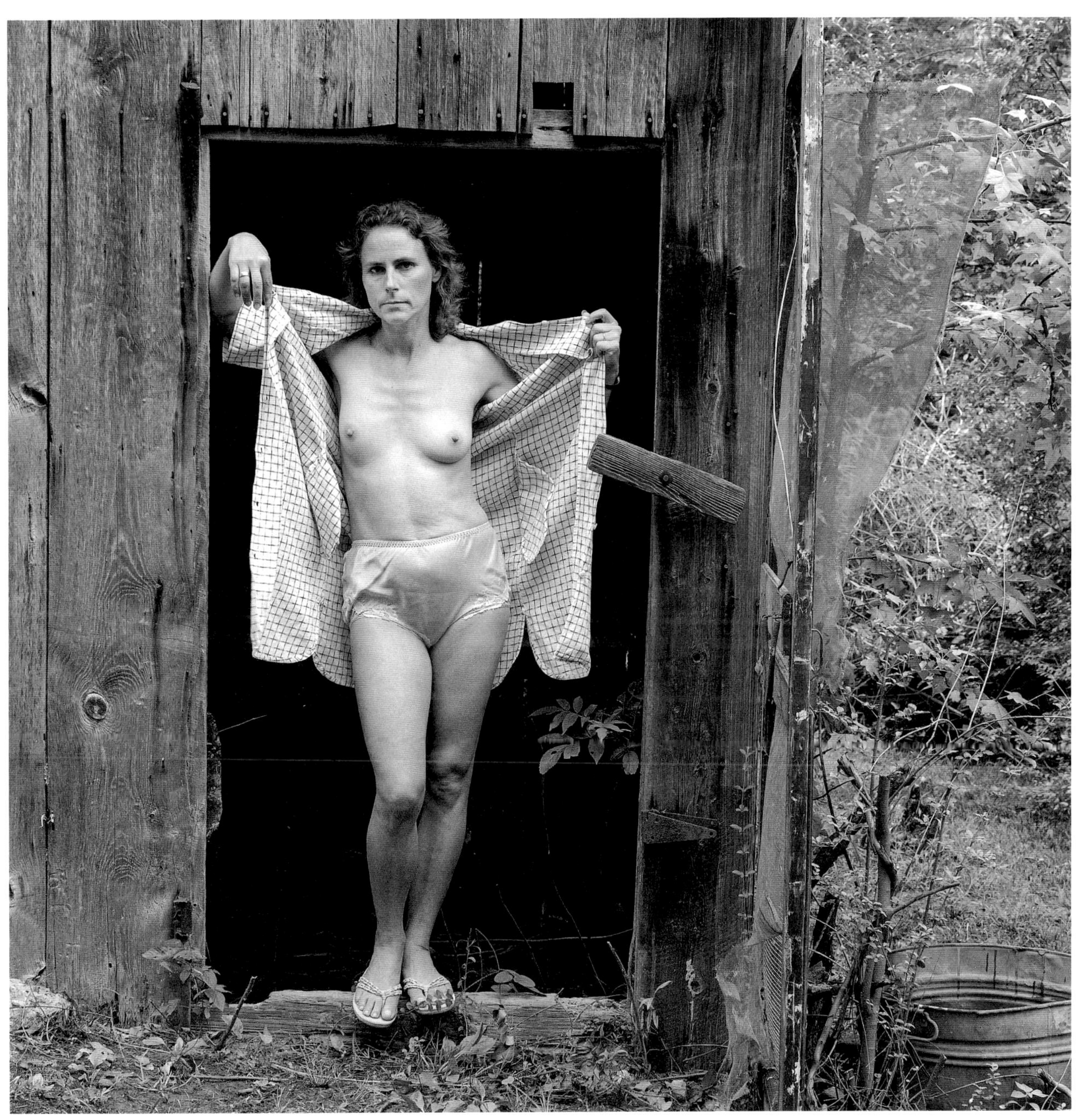

Edith, Danville, 1986

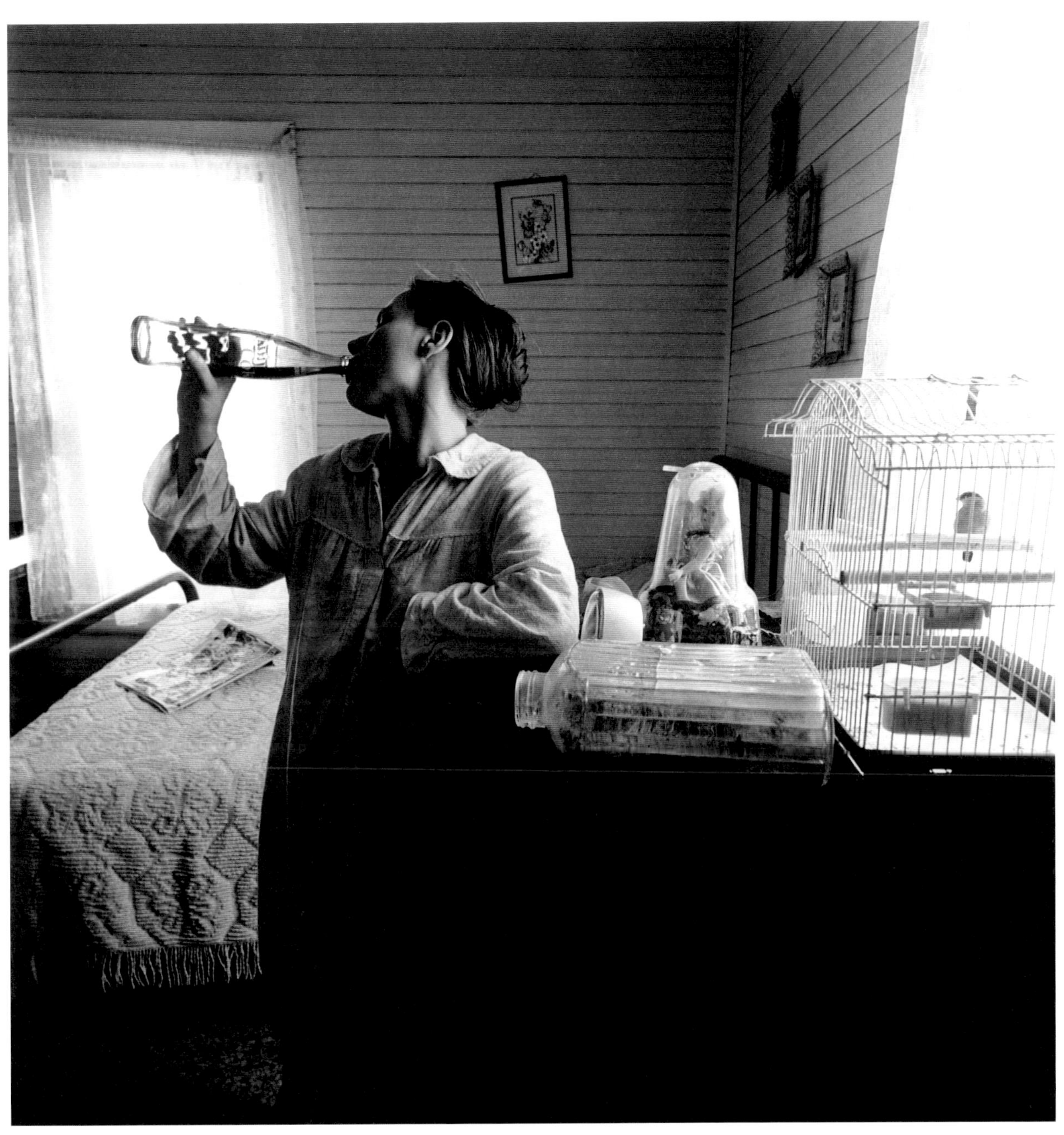

Edith, Danville, 1971

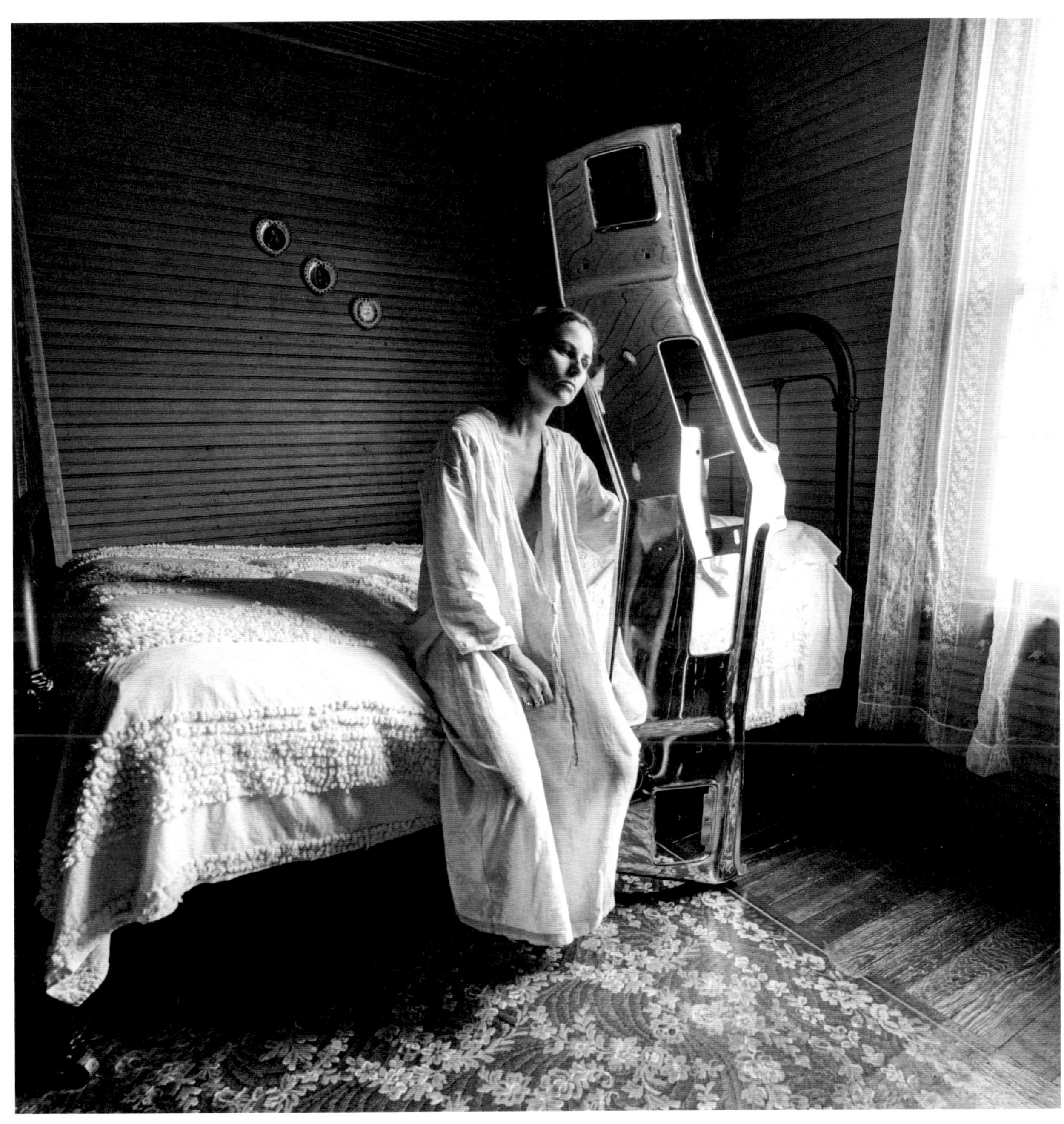

Edith, Danville, 1971

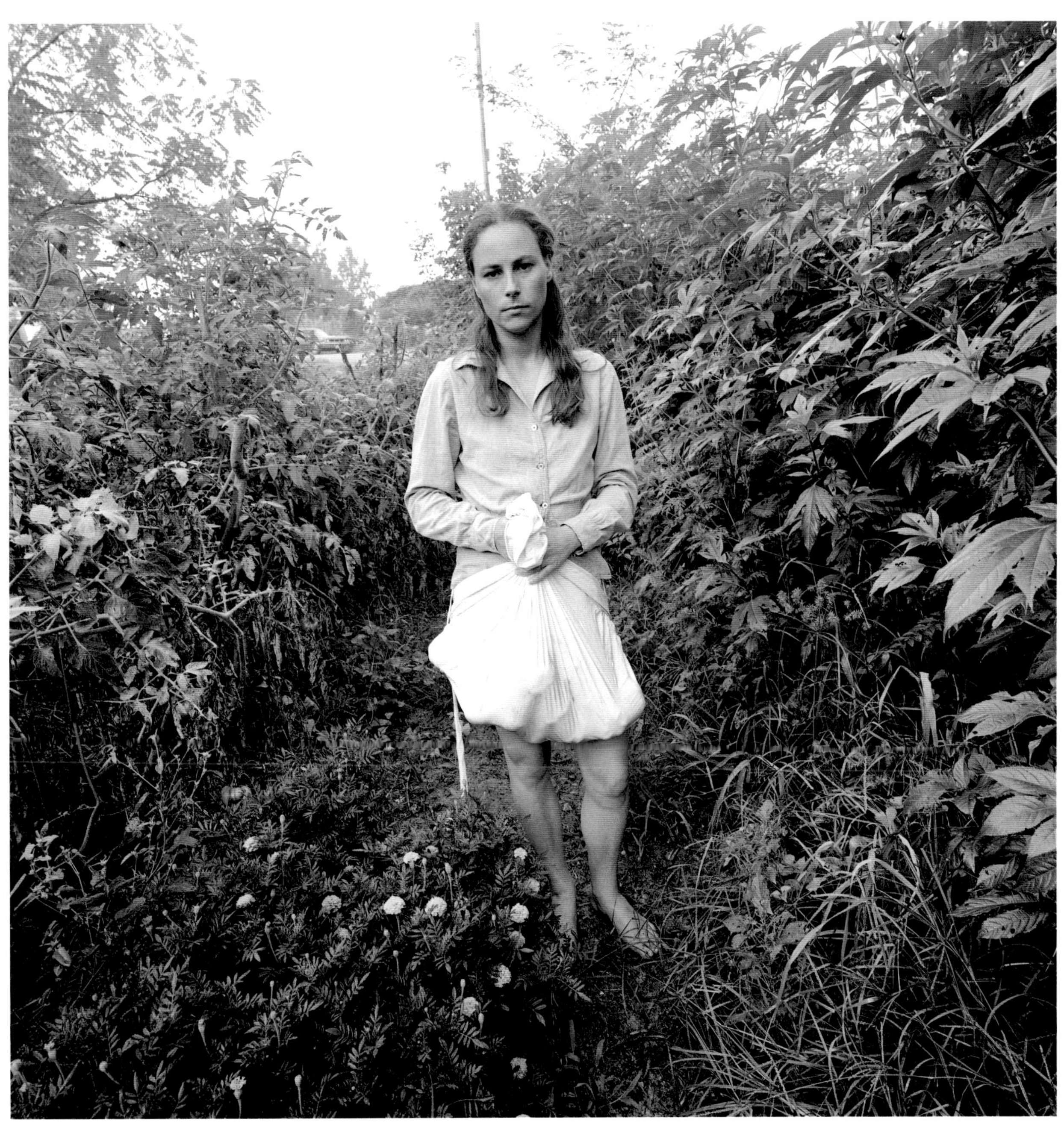

Edith, Danville, 1971

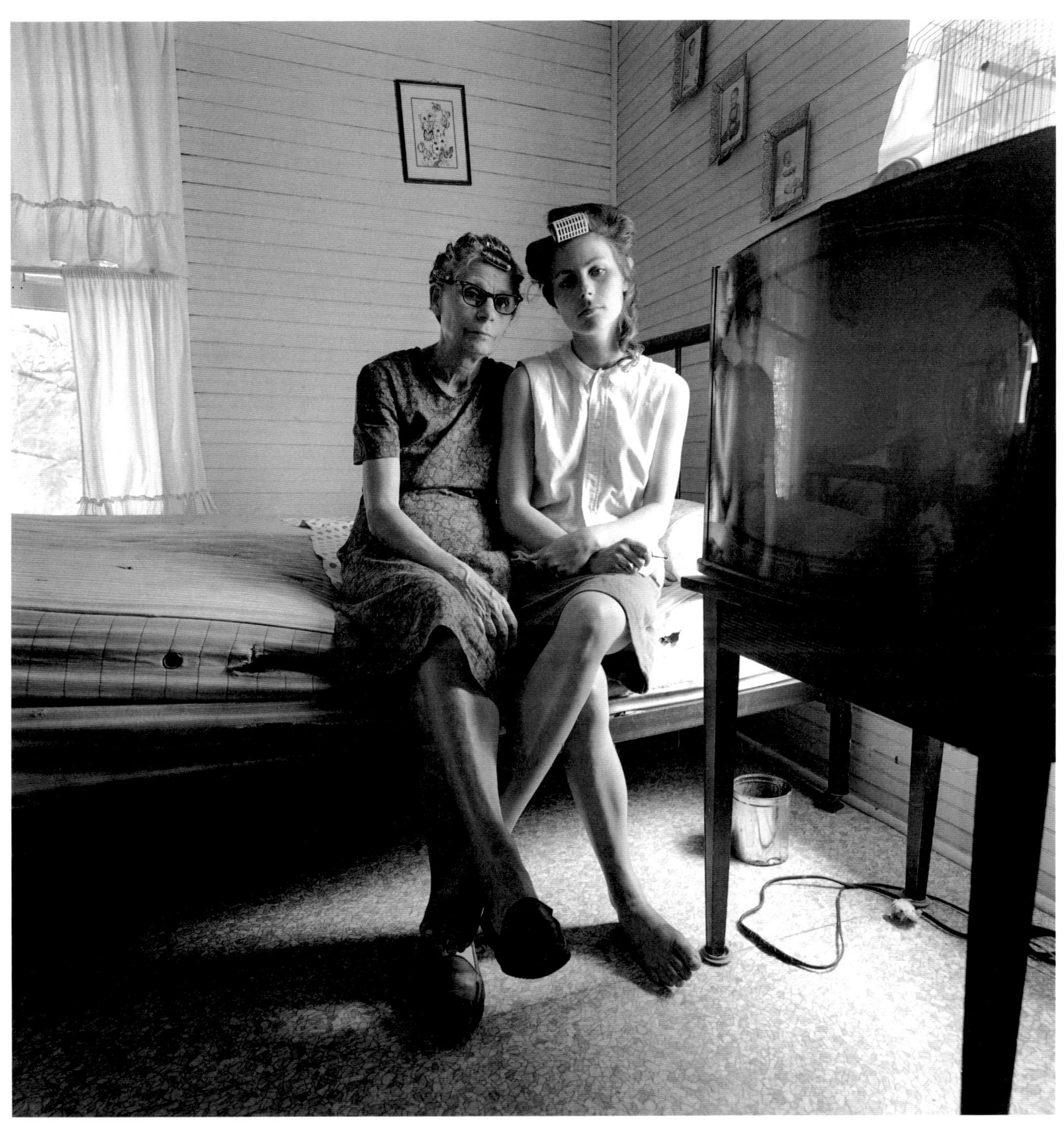

Reva and Edith, Danville, 1970

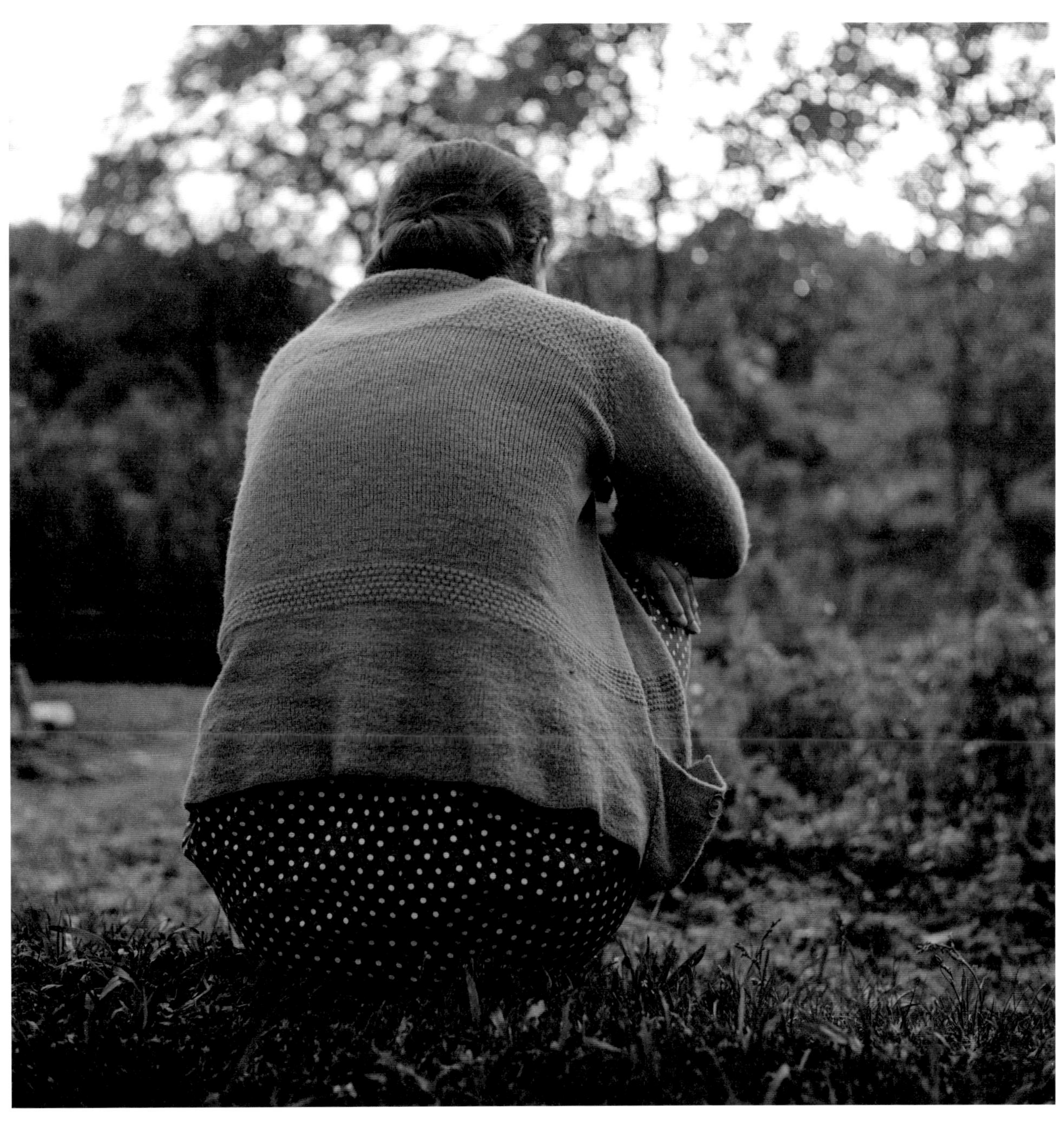

Edith, Danville, 1971

There are two versions of this, two negatives. In one, she turned her head to the side. She had called me over. She'd found that quilt and hung it up and then poked herself through it and said, "Come, come take a picture of this." I always loved her face and the folded arms but the best parts were in two different negatives. Then I couldn't put them together. And then a couple of summers ago, I was looking at it and I scanned both negatives. And once I'd done it, I realized they were now all in one file. I simply borrowed the extra set of arms.

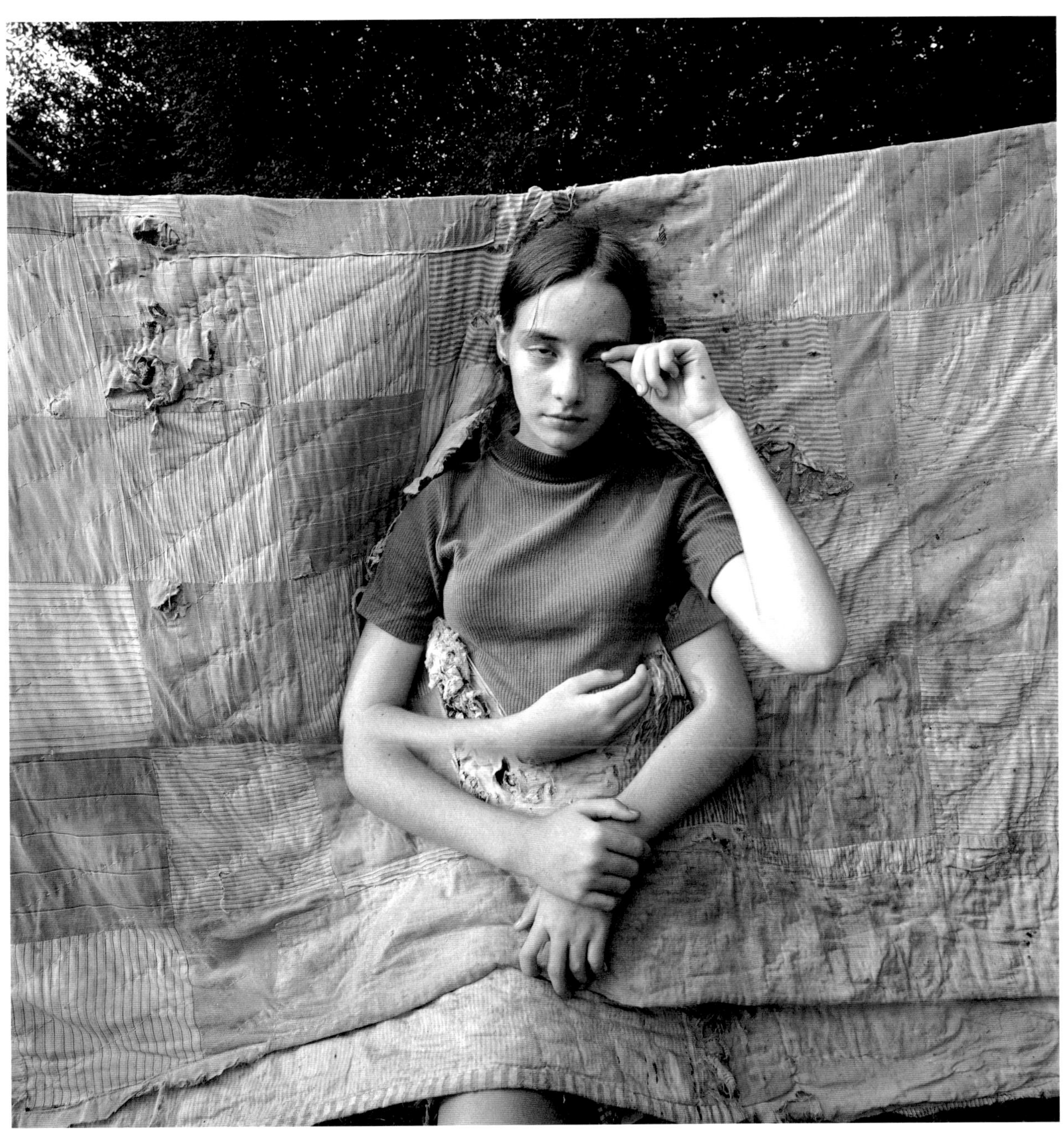

Nancy, Danville, 1973

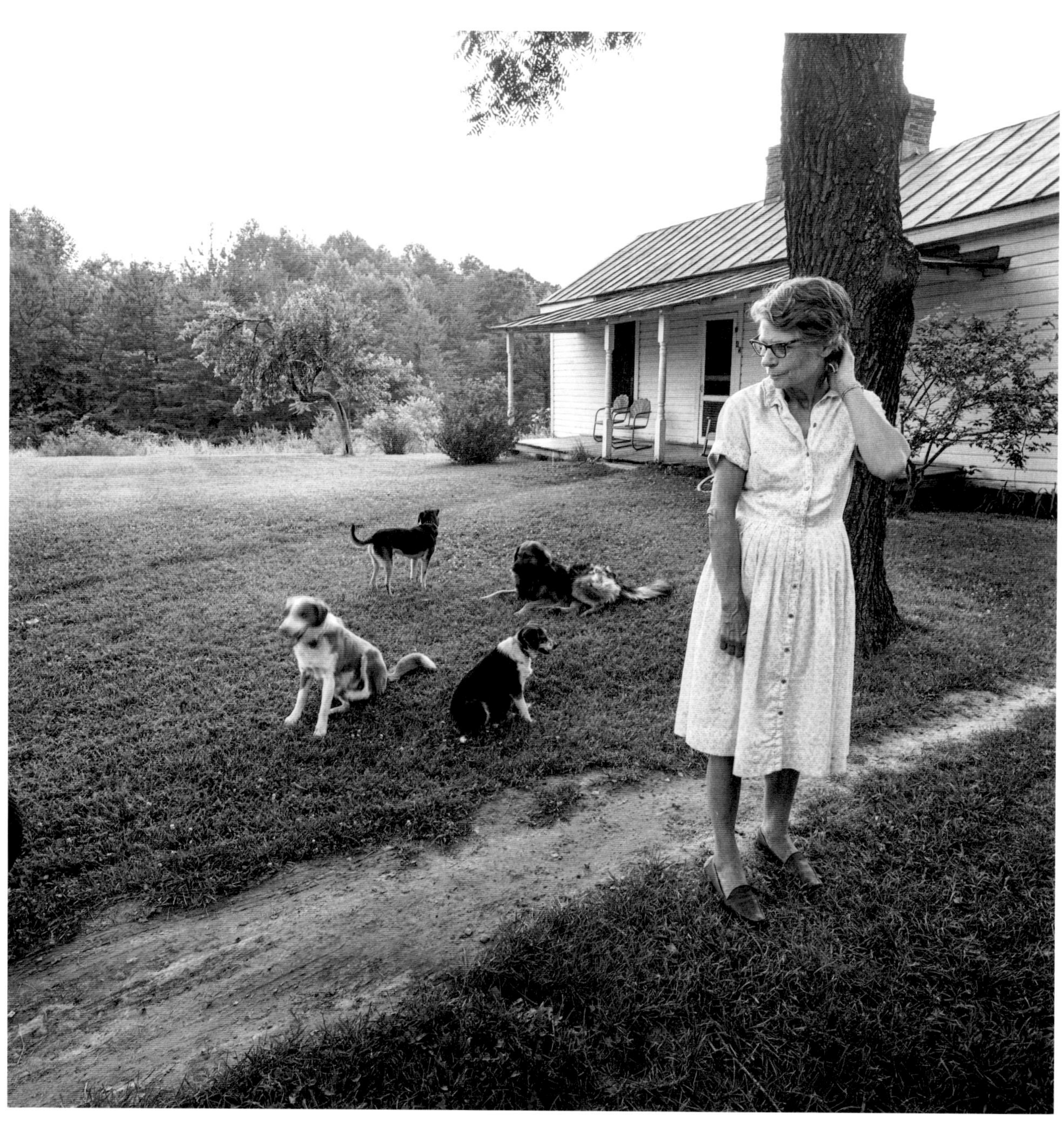

Reva in Front of Her Mother's House, Danville, 1971

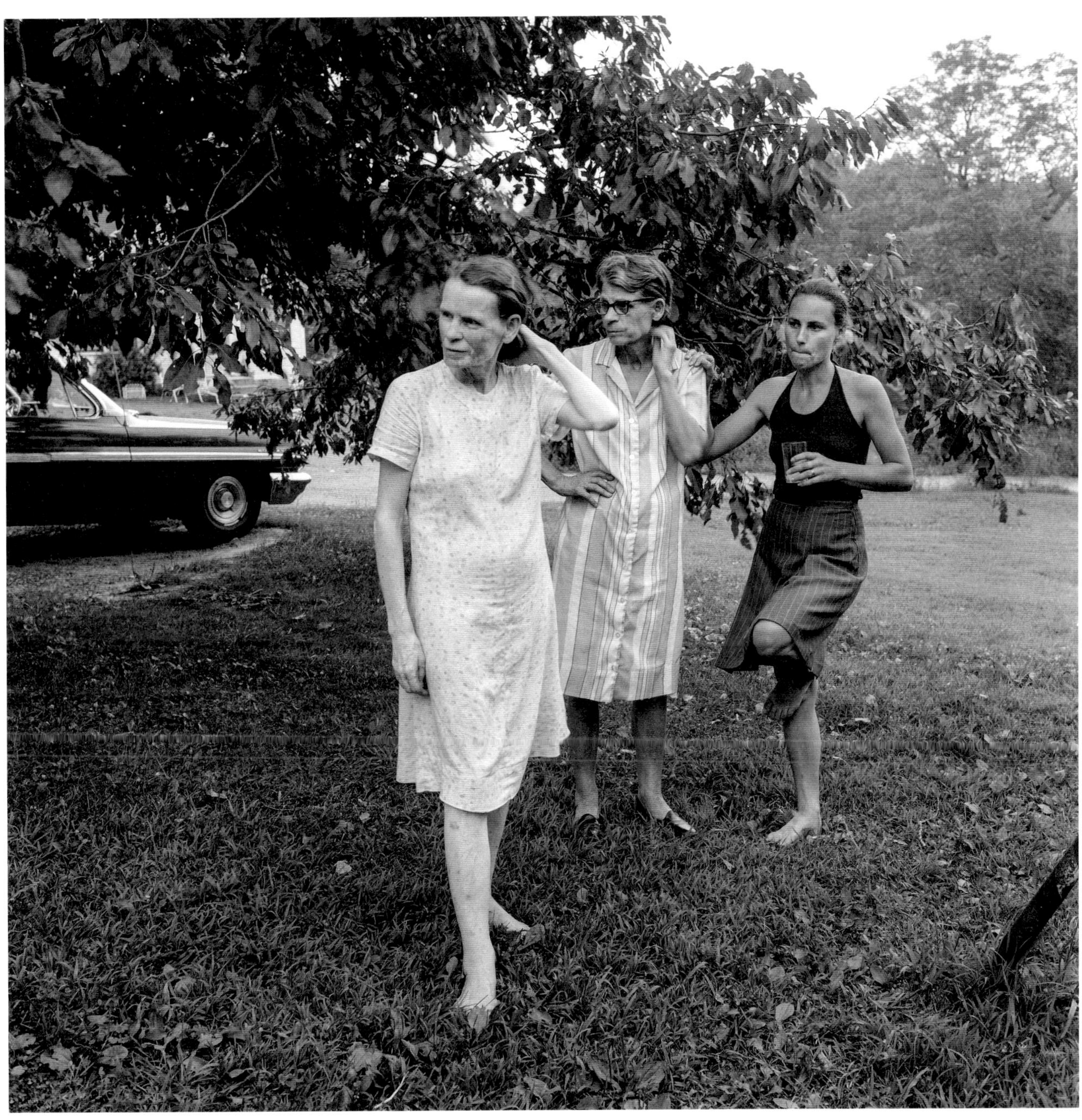

Maggie, Reva, and Edith, Danville, 1972

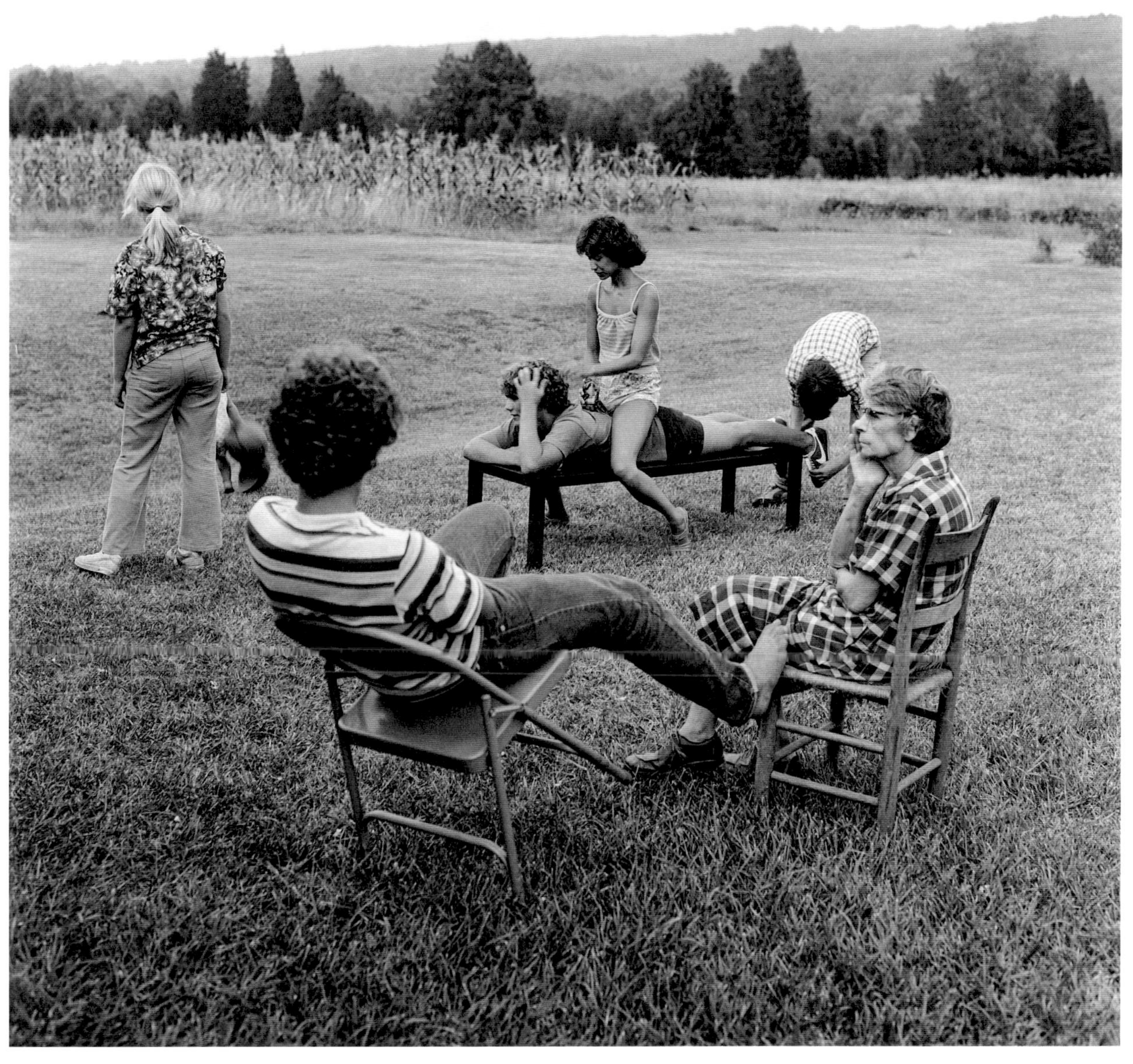

Family, Chatham, Virginia, 1981

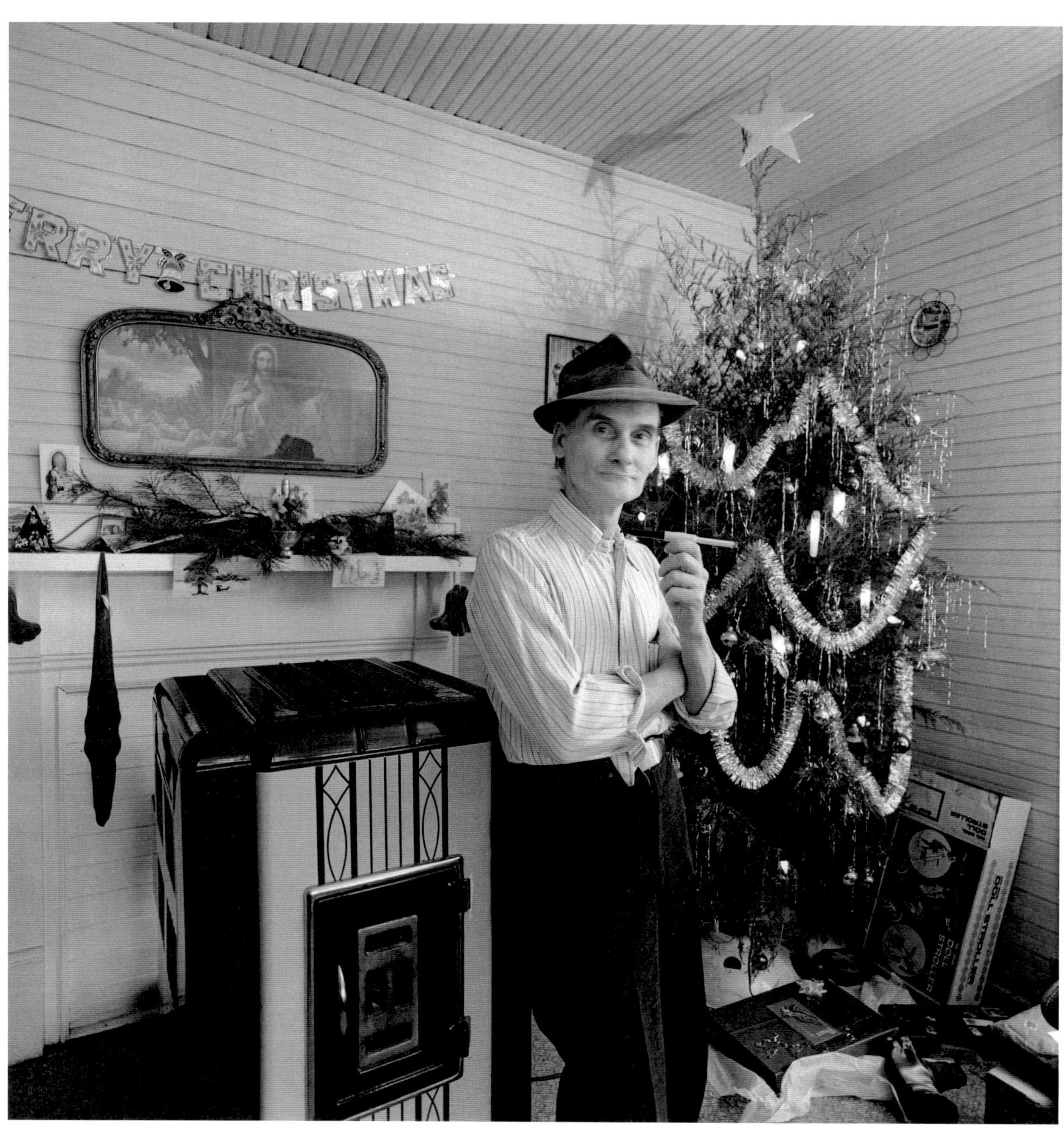

Ralph, Danville, 1970

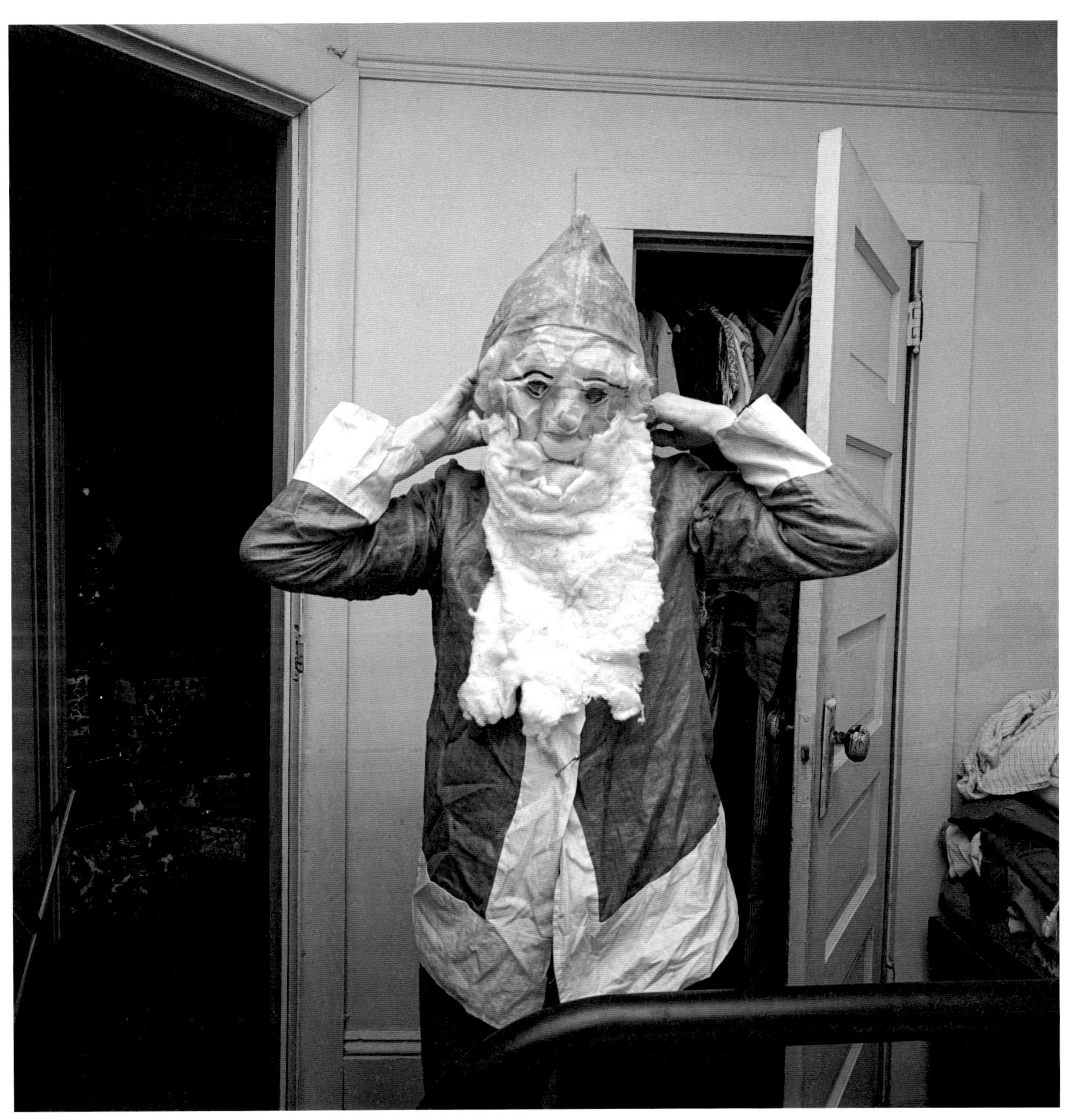

Maggie as Santa, Christmas, Danville, 1972

Sisters—Reva, Fanny, Bernice, and Gertrude. They made all their own dresses, and from the same gingham fabric they wove in the cotton mill.

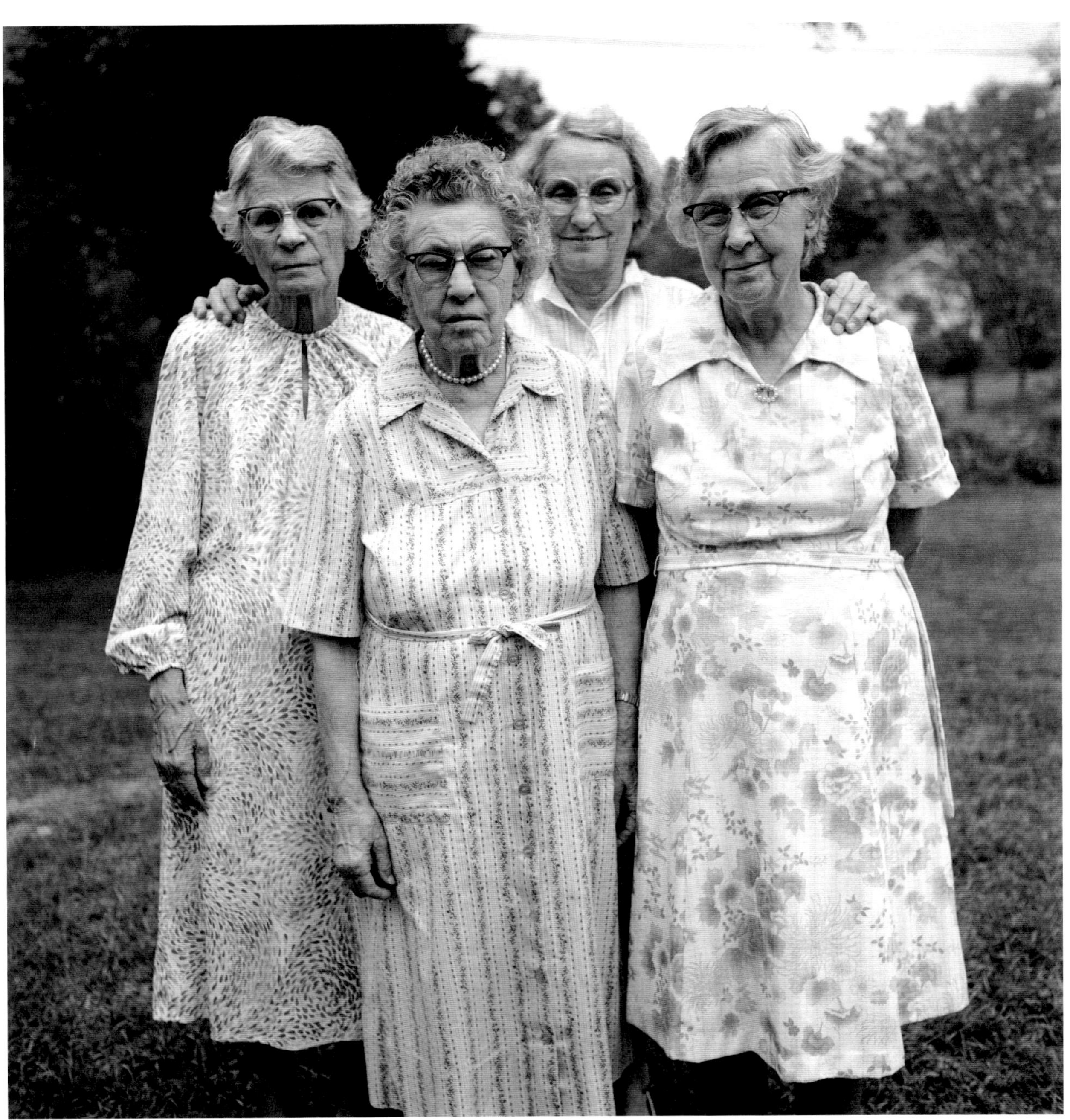

The Booher Sisters: Reva, Fannie, Bernice, and Gertrude, Danville, 1986

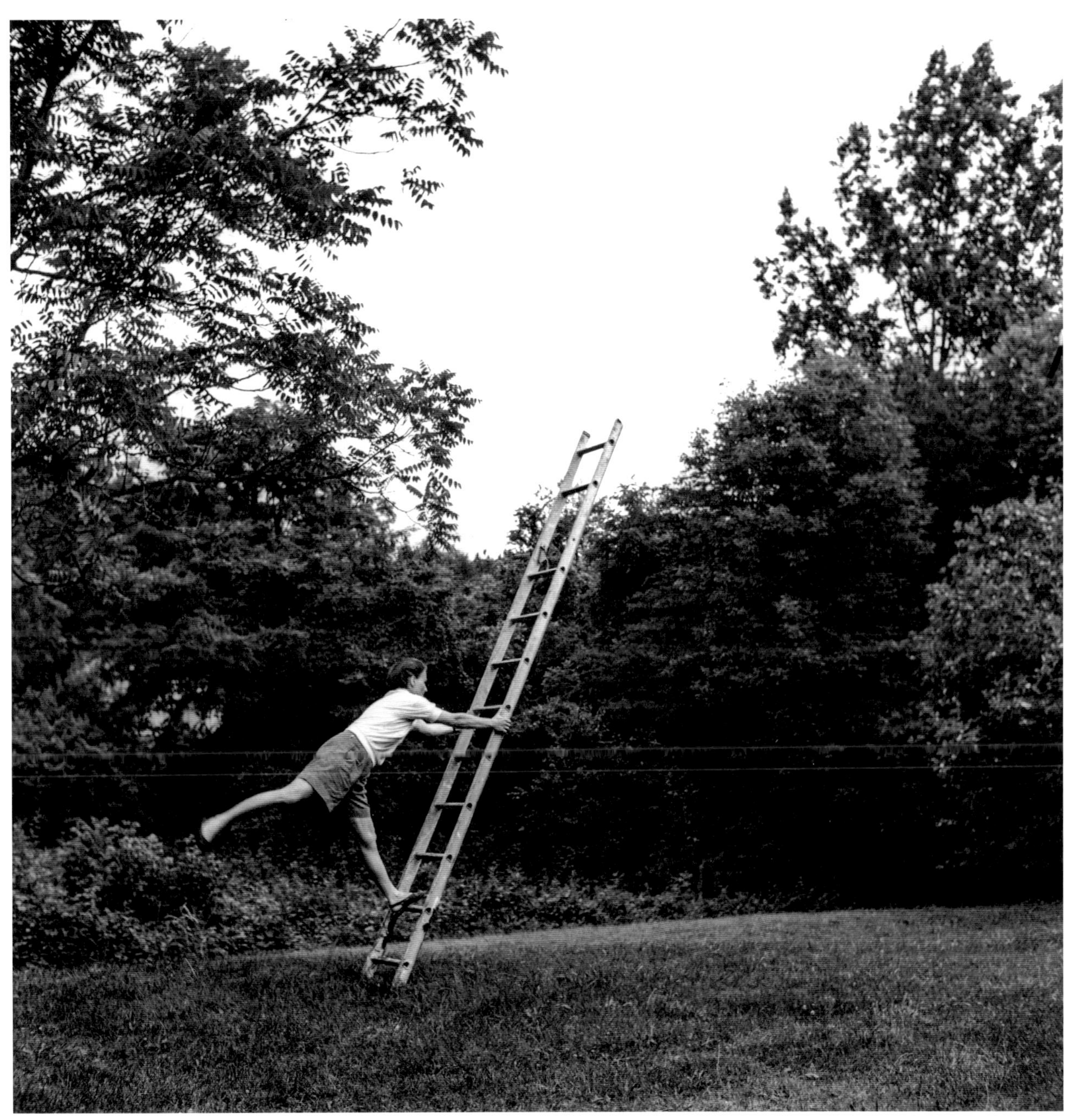

Edith, Danville, 1991

For Reva Morris, and for all those dear people who once lived on Baldwin Street
and for those who still do.
With warmest thanks to our friend Jane P. Watkins for her support and enthusiasm.

Published by Princeton University Press, 41 William Street, Princeton, New Jersey 08540
In the United Kingdom: Princeton University Press, 99 Banbury Road, Oxford OX2 6JX

GPSR Authorized Representative: Easy Access System Europe—
Mustamäe tee 50, 10621 Tallinn, Estonia, gpsr.requests@easproject.com

press.princeton.edu

Cover: Reva and Edith, Danville, 1984

ISBN 978-0-691-29303-5
British Library Cataloging-in-Publication Data is available

Coordinated by Michelle Komie, Annie Miller, Steven Sears, and Mark Bellis
Designed and typeset in Garamond by Katy Homans
Digital Separations by Trifolio Printing
Printing by Trifolio Printing under the supervision of Massimo Tonolli

Printed in Italy

1 3 5 7 9 10 8 6 4 2